THE ART
OF THE MOTOR

THE ART
OF THE MOTOR

THE ART
OF THE MOTOR

Paul Virilio

Translated by Julie Rose

 University of Minnesota Press
Minneapolis
London

The University of Minnesota gratefully acknowledges the funding provided by the French Ministry of Culture for the translation of this book.

Originally published as *L'art du moteur.*
Copyright 1993 Editions Galilée, Paris

Published by the University of Minnesota Press
111 Third Avenue South, Suite 290
Minneapolis, MN 55401-2520
Printed in the United States of America on acid-free paper

Third printing 1996

Library of Congress Cataloging-in-Publication Data

Virilio, Paul.
    [Art du moteur. English]
    The art of the motor / Paul Virilio ; translated by Julie Rose.
        p.   cm.
    Includes bibliographical references and index.
    ISBN 0-8166-2570-0 (hc). —ISBN 0-8166-2571-9 (pb)
    1. Information technology.   1. Title.
T58.5.V5713   1995
303.48'33—dc20   95-13845

This story, this episode, this adventure,
call it what you will.

CONRAD

CONTENTS

THE MEDIA COMPLEX

See all, hear all,
then forget.

NAPOLÉON

THE INDUSTRIAL MEDIA BENEFIT FROM a curious depravity in the laws of democracy. If television and, by osmosis, the press are not at liberty a priori to provide false information, our legislation on the other hand grants them the exorbitant power of lying by omission, by censuring or ruling out news that does not suit them or that might damage their interests.

The *fourth estate*—still the agreed term—is thus the only one of our institutions that can function outside any effective democratic control, since the public at large does not get to hear any independent criticism of the media, or of any possible alternative, simply because such criticism does not stand a chance of being broadcast widely and of consequently reaching the general public.

A few years ago, an international conference on the freedom of the press acknowledged this fact, drawing the following conclusion:

Freedom of the press and 'the other media remains an ideal. No one can limit its field, or define with any degree of precision who might actually possess this freedom.[1]

The masses are seriously in the dark when it comes to the mass media, so if it is true that in a democracy everyone has a right to information within the provisions of the law, it would seem that the fourth estate lies outside the law or above laws, the latter coming up short right where the media's real field of power begins. This *paraconstitutional* position of the large-scale industrial media can be explained quite simply, however. Montaigne claimed that laws *are based on customs dictated by the fluctuating sea of a people's or a prince's opinions.* If this is so, then the mass media, which enjoy the power of managing information and thereby of whipping up the fluctuating sea of public opinion, would have a field day with social customs and morals and with them the whole set of vague rules and prohibitions that go to make up legislation they have secretly been inventing for ages. This happens under any and every political or economic regime.

Yet having in the past two hundred years reached an apogee from where *it decrees the law,* the fourth estate is now witnessing the compromising of its splendid isolation. All the opinion polls point to this; rare are those who would still insist, as Thomas Jefferson once did, that the freedom of the media is *the most effective way to the truth* or that information processing is "objective."

Left to their own devices at the end of the age of dissuasion, the industrial media have gone the way of all mass production in recent years, from the necessary to the superfluous, to the ugly free-for-all of deregulation and increasingly ferocious internecine struggles. Their power to denounce, to reveal, to flaunt has been growing endlessly to the detriment of the now precarious privilege of dissimulation—so much so that currently the real problem of the press and television no longer lies in what they are able to show as much as in what they can still manage to obliterate, to hide. Until now, this constituted the essential nature of their power. "The media are not a fourth power, they are a counterpower," the journalist Jacques Derogy recently claimed. "They cause all that is opaque or secret to fade away."

A brave champion of investigative journalism, Derogy cannot seem to see the dangers of the general "bringing to the surface" that is threatening the small screen with extinction in the short term, just as it threatened the big screen twenty years ago—which at the time seemed unimaginable. In fact, if we are to believe filmmaker Ray Harryhausen, it is the *disappearance of censorship* that has gradually sterilized cinematographers' and viewers' imaginations before going on to bring down the commercial cinema, with theaters closing down and film studios being sold off all around the globe.

dissimulate
- manipulate truth
- change the facts

Television's position is similarly critical, with the anarchic proliferation of private, cable, and Hertzian channels and the spread of zapping. Things have degenerated since the abolition of the previous geopolitical limits of our field of vision with the unveiling, in the space of a few months, of a world till then hidden from the West's camera lenses, behind the opacity of the Iron Curtain or the Berlin Wall.

Against all the odds, the fourth dimension of *Live TV,* thought to be an extraordinary freeing of the media, would go on to seriously undermine media credibility. In other words, the very reality of the facts so smugly illuminated by the cameras; and this process would go as far as including any notion of media truth.

Less than two years after its international triumph in the Gulf War, CNN is in serious trouble; the *Wall Street Journal* of April 6, 1993, reveals that Ted Turner is having real financial difficulties.

Without visual limits there can be no, or almost no, mental imagery; without a certain blindness, no tenable appearance. To want the *total image* to triumph—the way the materialists, followed by the documentary makers of the turn of the century, dreamed about in relation to the "great object"; to desire that spectators be "equal before the image" as advertising agents once did, and then partisans of cathode tube democracy, "means to denude oneself before the ghosts. . . . It is on this ample nourishment that they multiply so enormously. . . . The ghosts won't starve, but we will perish," Kafka writes to Milena in 1922, a year before his own death.[2]

The question now is how far the media can compromise themselves with the *nouveau spectaculaire* arising from the urgency of real-time technologies and that has now infiltrated the entire network of mass communications, in the West as in the East, spreading its net indifferently across political, economic, social, or legal information to the pseudoentertainment, freed from any form of censorship, that includes *live talk shows,* video clips, pornography, and interactive games.

Aware of the specific risk the mass media are running, an English press baron named Andreas Whittam Smith launched a preemptive strike at the end of the 1980s. Smith drew up a *deontological chart* in which every case scenario was carefully examined: the circumstances in which invasion of privacy is permissible, the issue of material, under-the-counter benefits, and, in particular, the *extent of right of reply.*[3]

Smith's initiative was quickly followed by eleven other English newspapers, as well as *El Pais* and *La Repubblica* shortly after. This was no sudden bout of puritanism. It was about dealing with what was most pressing while preserving the institution's principal prerogative at all costs: *the power to dissimulate.*

"British journalists today have as bad an image as bookmakers and politicians," the same A. W. Smith asserts before coming to the point. "Two years ago, we were afraid that a law would be introduced that would make *right of reply* compulsory for every critical article, if papers continued to go it alone without publishing their professional code of ethics."

Smith remains convinced that *the fourth estate cannot be divided.* No doubt he has not forgotten that in the beginning MEDIATIZATION was the opposite of COMMUNICATIONS; it was a relic of feudal barbarity, of ancient ostracism. Up until the twentieth century, to be MEDIATIZED meant literally being stripped of one's IMMEDIATE RIGHTS. The emperor Napoléon I thus mediatized certain hereditary princes as he conquered them, depriving them of their freedom to move or make decisions while leaving them the appearance of a power they were no longer in a position to exercise. Just after the Second World War, the "satellization" of Eastern European countries by the Soviet Union revived this particularly perverse practice. Napoléon, the great "mediatizer" who finally ran out of time, was the master of the swift victory, of the military campaign based on speed and surprise—shock tactics. It almost goes without saying, though it is a little-known fact, that Napoléon founded the industrial press in France, indirectly engendering what would become a modern *communications complex.*

This was a system originally set up for information gathering, investigation, and censorship with the help of police minister Joseph Fouché and his disciples, such as the famous Charles Louis Havas. It also had the financial backing of Gabriel Julien Ouvrard, the dubious banker who tendered for army supplies.[4]

Theoretical force behind the Terror, Saint-Just once asserted that, "Whenever a people can be put down, they are." Today it would be no exaggeration to say that, "Whenever a people can be mediatized, they are!"

This being the case, we should be looking at the industrialization and massive commercialization of our communication tools as much as at the proliferation of our nuclear arms—and their joint race for ubiquity and instantaneity.

When it is less a matter of determining at what distance broadcast "reality" lies, than at what speed its image can be displayed on our screens, we might indeed wonder if the industrial media have not reached a threshold of tolerance more *ethological* than deontological. Can the media distance themselves indefinitely from the "natural" conditions of communication, from the balance between demand and capability that is its basis?

Everyone knows that for human beings, as for every living species, the *ability to communicate* is the indispensable condition of *being in the world,* that is, of survival. It is an innate ability that normally enables us to distinguish between our immediate environment and the representations we make of it, our mental imagery.

Along with this primary ability to adapt to the world-in-motion that surrounds us, we have the even more complex ability to distinguish between what we think is real and therefore true, and what another individual might consider real and true. Through language (gestural, vocal, graphic), this secondary ability allows us to *put ourselves in the other person's place, to see with his or her eyes,* to take advantage of his or her optical system to be warned of an event, to *re-present* to ourselves people and objects we cannot see or cannot yet see, and to finally act accordingly.

"Natural" communication therefore demands audiovisual proximity and fairly restricted intervals or territory; it also demands a limited number of communicants, each sharing the same vocalizations or other semantic signals.[5]

Until fairly recently, our modes of knowledge and representation (in the arts and sciences, religion, war, social and sexual activity, and so on) depended as much on ourselves (our own bodies) as on the incredible ability to double up by identifying with the *alter ego*, literally, this *other me* that allowed us to "see," or rather conceive, the real at a distance and that meant our point of view had *a natural social relief*. A bit the way the slight gap between one's eyes produces the depth of the image one perceives, its *stereoscopy*, thanks to the slight spatiotemporal lag in ocular motility.

But let's go back to Marcel Pagnol's reflection, which I've so often quoted elsewhere. In theater, each member of the audience scattered throughout the auditorium necessarily sees a different play. In the cinema, on the other hand, these same spectators see exactly what the camera has seen, wherever they happen to be sitting; that is, they see *the same film*. Pagnol goes so far as to conclude that in a room with a thousand spectators there is really *only one*.

The projector, designed to optically replace the *alter ego* (the other me) by enabling the viewer glued to his seat to see as *present* what is naturally *absent* and outside the restricted circle of their visual reach, in fact eliminates the stereoscopic couple that previously composed and gave life to the social depth of the real. The great documentary filmmaker François Reichenbach had this to say on the disappearance of the "active perceiving being": "Having a camera changed my life. With it, through it, I could project a different way of looking at everything."

From the "armament" of the photographic camera to the "armed eye" of the reporter or soldier, in anticipation of the police surveillance video, the camera lense has violently drawn the human eye to different beings and things simply because, as Wisemann tells us, *new technologies make this possible.* "From the moment I owned a camera," Reichenbach goes on to say, "*I no longer felt the slightest interest in being with people, in living among them, unless I could get them on film.*"

The camera would forever after come between him and all things; the miracle of industrial cinema lay in reproducing this primordial communication breakdown by the million.

Dziga Vertov ("the man with a camera") wrote, "I am the machine that shows you the world *as I alone see it.*" This machine plunges inert cinemagoers into an unprecedented form of solitude, *multiple solitude,* since, as Marcel Pagnol so aptly puts it, a thousand spectators are reduced to one in the cinema auditorium! At the beginning of the 1960s, Marshall McLuhan contrasted the screen with the written word and claimed that television, after radio, had restored immediacy and a universal resonance that the book had discarded in favor of a sequential sense of the world.

If, as Gaboriau claimed, *time is just one more obscurity,* effacing material indices one by one and removing us from the reality of facts and things, then what can we say about the reality effect of time-light, of the false proximity of this world without density or shadow whose promised unification had McLuhan drooling?

At the end of the 1950s, Fidel Castro decided to appeal directly to American advertising agencies to promote the Cuban Revolution. Later, during the *Balance of Terror, private terrorism,* encouraged principally by a communist block anxious to destabilize Western nations, imposed its *data power* by furiously churning out documentaries, thereby ensuring that restricted groups and asocial minorities had powerful media coverage. It is estimated, for instance, that a billion people watched the unfolding of the Munich Olympic Games in 1972 and were thereby "present" at the Palestinian commando's massacre of the Israeli athletes.

When the Eastern bloc disintegrated, the great military groups were seen to splinter into a host of national, ethnic, and economic ghettos, heavily armed and soon to take over from *private terrorism,* with mass killers, snipers, and sundry *tchekniks.* They were also to take up a *nuclear anticity strategy,* this time playing to the cameras, showing the systematic destruction and "cleansing" of historic villages; the taking hostage of minorities; the murder, broadcast live, of innocent people in Romania, Iraq, Sarajevo, Kosovo. . . .

By way of some "world-city," the intensive implementation of communication technologies has certainly created waves—the unforeseen ones of the camera effect signaled by Pagnol, which now extends *multiple solitude* to billions of individuals, the counterculture of the (postindustrial, postnational, posturban) ghetto now spreading over the whole of a planet that cannot manage to shake off its status as the ghetto of the cosmos.

From the ghetto comes the chaos that destabilizes mass media caught in the trap of the internal act of war, the violation of human rights—the fascinating spectacle, endlessly replayed, of immolation and a long, slow death.

Surely it is impossible not to see the similarity between ethnic cleansing in Eastern Europe and the critical situation in the marginalized urban wastelands of the West's metropolises where faceless vandalism, drugs, prostitution, racketeering, and armed combat between racial gangs have become commonplace; or between these and the devastation of former colonies now in the throes of military anarchy, famine, and tribal massacre. Do we really need to remind ourselves that thirty years ago, American television was already considered the main reason for "the upward mobility revolution" in the United States? According to the experts, by insistently exposing the luxury goods of consumer society in movies or promotional lotteries, the preferred medium of disinherited minorities was the chief cause of the bloody rioting that broke out in the South's ghettos before spreading north to Detroit and Newark in 1967. Television's responsibility was further aggravated by its own reports of the troubles, black leaders like Stokely Carmichael or Rap Brown having had few emulators until radio and television stations gave them hours of airtime every day and made veritable stars of them.

So after creating it in the first place, television then fueled the violence it was supposed to be elucidating to the public—just by the mere presence of TV cameras at the scene of the confrontations, murder, and looting.[6] This interactivity between "advertising" and information rapidly incited militants and student leaders to follow the example of ethnic minorities. To draw media attention to the university ghetto, all you had to do was set fire to or occupy the student campus, which was exactly what they did, duly imitated by student bodies here and there throughout the world. The ever-growing mass of social rejects soon made a habit of such procedures.

With *glasnost,* Western television was given the opportunity to act at a distance on the inhabitants of the East, just as the pariahs of the American ghettos had done thirty years before, by exasperating desires born of being shut out, of frustration and social suffering. It then finished off its universal job by broadcasting images of popular uprisings, real or simulated, twenty-four hours a day, thus helping to quickly fan the fire—right up until Moscow's "hunger riots" of August 1991.

During the riots, international television broadcast a spectacular episode in real time. On the night of August 22, in the light of powerful projectors, the crowds of Moscow unbolted and tipped over the colossal statue of Felix Dzerzinski that stood opposite the ex-KGB buildings.

This joker died in 1926; in his day, he had been head of secret Soviet diplomacy and genial mastermind of *strategic disinformation,* which he summed up in one sentence:

"Westerners take what they want for reality, so let's give them what they want!"

Did we really have to let ourselves be had yet again by the televisual theatrics surrounding the overturning of the bronze colossus? Was the Soviet dream that night a shattered illusion and the dream of the West an illusion that would survive the end of the age of dissuasion?

For a long time, confronted by the fearful communist disinformation machine, the capitalist world also excelled in taking what it wanted for reality.

Advertising had gingerly reared its head at the beginning of the nineteenth century under the "news in brief" rubric before being hoisted up to the level of financial partner destined, it was thought, to ensure the material and moral freedom of the press at little cost. Over time, advertising was to attain industrial status and carve out a dominant niche for itself at the very heart of the communications industry.

Just after the nationalization of the Soviet media and well before the New Deal of the 1930s, American consumer society kicked off—creating with it the need for *mass marketing*—marketing capable of leveling cultural, economic, geographic, and ethnic differences. This meant state intervention in the social and industrial spheres, followed promptly by the appropriate authorities secretly getting their hands on photographic, film, and radio agencies.

Afterward, the term *publicity* would mean "*propaganda*." In the United States it would evolve from simple promotion of consumer goods to more general information, the latter gradually eluding existential journalists and falling to the lot of the advertising industry and its various agents.

The new complex first successfully tackled the American domestic market before attempting to penetrate Europe, in vain, up until the Second World War. *Beating an enemy involves not so much capturing as captivating them.* The economic battlefield would soon blur into the field of military perception, and the project of the American communications complex would then become explicit: it would aim at world mediatization.

Less than a year after the explosion at Hiroshima, American secretary of state James Byrnes managed to wrest an important financial contract from the aging Léon Blum. The contract contained an "appendix" whose reach the French did not quite grasp, involving as it did relinquishing most of the mechanisms protecting the French film industry from its American competitors, with picture theaters in France no longer having to screen more than one French film a month. The accord brought about a collapse in the quality and vitality of French cinema.

Since 1986, subsequent to the negotiations of the Uruguay Round, the free-traders of the GATT, at the behest of the United States, have pushed for further expansion of their capacities to include the *services trade,* which they argue ought to encompass *the cultural and the audiovisual—* that is, 35 percent of world trade. In Europe, the image market is already 70 percent American-dominated; in Africa, over 90 percent.[7]

At the end of the 1980s, a little late in the day, a certain French advertiser could thus claim that *advertising is democracy,* landing himself a chair as member of the Académie Française for his pains. Since traditional political discourse has become a dead language, adding to the limbo of disinformation an intellectual discourse that is also running out of steam, why should an advertising executive not take a spot under the Coupole, next to the cardinals and marshals, the men of science and letters, of the film industry and the press; why should the language of advertising not be consecrated in turn as yet another academic discourse?

Closely tied in with state propaganda, and accused of immorality by its detractors—in particular consumer-protection groups (should one have the legal right to tempt citizens to such an extent, all the better to disappoint them?)—advertising certainly managed to saturate all spheres of power without fear or favor, from sport to science, philosophy, ethics, culture, humanitarian aid. To say nothing of the pressure it exerts on the democratic state itself thanks to the psychologically enfeebled condition of the parliamentary world. It has got to the stage where members of the powerful Washington lobby can claim to be ready to "be involved in the search for solutions to all the problems confronting the American people." This is a population in which each individual is subjected on average to more than fifteen hundred ads a day in explicit, hidden, or subliminal form.[8]

Similarly, the endlessly expanding volume of the export market in "services" controlled by the American advertising industry (films, cassette tapes, revues, compact discs) can come to seem to free-traders like L. T. Steele "the way to go in building the world of the future"!

A certain director of the French TV station TF1 said recently:

> In television, the dividing line between programs and in-formation is less and less clear. . . . But the main news broadcast is strongly demarcated and it is the exclusive province of journalists. The rest is an intermediate zone; info is slipped in almost anywhere except for game shows. There is no boundary, certainly not as far as the public is concerned, between information and the rest of the program. So when we had a big show to propose, we wanted to give it to Anne Sinclair and Christophe Dechavanne—a journalist and a game show presenter. That's the best kind of example of the harmony that should exist within a channel.

A message like this can be decoded by replacing the term *information* with *information complex*. At a time when a simple ban on cigarette or alcohol advertising is threat-ening to wipe out most of the periodicals of the written press as well as certain private TV channels, it seems that the *commercial break* and the *news break* constitute a perfect paradigm. There is no clear dividing line anywhere; over the years the whole of television production has been gradually sliding into this *intermediate zone* governed exclusively by economic constraints. As for Sinclair and Dechavanne, we all know that individual personalities just keep going down the cathode gurgler, so-called entertainers liable to be sent packing at a moment's notice like any old domestic appliance that no longer works. Sinclair, in any case, is not, strictly speaking, a journalist inasmuch as she is not in a position to ensure any follow-up whatsoever of news items. This being the case, why not indeed throw such specimens together?

A journalist recently asked Maurice Levy, head of the old Publicis agency, "Isn't advertising facing a sort of crisis of confidence, as much as politics and the media?"

In the United States, *the networks,* which used to have an 80 percent stake in expenditure on national TV advertising campaigns, have seen their hegemony undermined in recent times. Having leaped from $4 billion in 1947 to more than $25 billion from the 1960s onward, the annual turnover of the American advertising industry is also continually being seriously eroded.

As soon as this crisis of confidence arose, certain Italian advertisers decided it was time to rip the gloves off and once more ask the fundamental question: *who is mediatizing whom these days?* Given the state of decay of a consumer society doomed to disappear without much further ado, it became urgent to readjust the now anachronistic ad/info duo: due to the impact of *Live TV,* international terrorism offers the news a large stock of stunning images capable of mediatizing the crowd very cheaply. Advertising could thus borrow terrorism's aesthetic, revulsion taking over from attraction and the pseudoseductions of those *show-off* 1980s video clips, which were both expensive and ineffectual.

Luciano Benetton took note: "People are smarter than advertisers. They live in the real world."

Taking a leaf from terrorism's book, advertising would rush to make official its status as *a major communications player*. Like terrorism, it would destroy the last remaining taboos, complacently presenting suffering, agony, death, and ecological disaster . . . and attacking democracy, art, politics, and religion. Anne Magnien, coproducer of *Culture-Pub*, notes in April 1992, "Benetton has found *a chink in the media armour*; he reckons the media are no longer performing their role as relay *in public awareness,* and you'd better believe him. Brand names depend on the marketing of values lacking in our institutions. . . . Commercial failure is the most effective sanction, more moral than that of any censor."

What "morality" could this mean if not that of the end, of the eschatology of social communication? After thirty years of audiovisual activity, the communications network faces a new equation: *a person = a ghetto*. Radio and television now only address the anomic mass they have helped create, that great inextricable social morass whose protagonists survive as best they can in *multiple solitude*—marginals; divorced singles; the unemployed; members of ethnic, sexual, or health minorities; children of single parents left to their own devices. The mass media, with their democratic ambitions, seem to have reached the point of no return, a threshold of tolerance where their specific powers dim as other kinds of dependencies, more solitary, more close to the bone, rise to the fore. This is the case with the children of the ghettos of America, clutching at drugs, pornography, and murder and contemptuously relegating television and the press to oldsters and whites only.

Advertising agent Philippe Michel once said, "Ads are not supposed to make things sell, they are supposed to create attitudes." What is now known as the *advertorial* started off with rock videos but, more particularly, with antialcohol, antismoking, and antidrug campaigns. As Charles Manson attested, "If you hadn't told me drugs existed, I never would have taken them." We do not, in fact, know of any advertising campaign that turns people off anything whatsoever!

The same thing applies when, in 1993, for the requirements of a major women's magazine, an elegantly attired "beauty queen" is filmed running through the ruins of Sarajevo among stoved-in cars, imitating the fatal flight of the town's inhabitants as snipers open fire on them. The sight line of the fashion photographer then becomes completely indistinguishable from that of the assassin lying in wait. It is his solitary excitement we are invited to share.

During the last world war, propaganda services shunned this kind of effect simply because they believed peace would probably be restored; they therefore had to bear in mind peace's most precious symbols, such as prosperity, culture, sport, entertainment, and the family. In contrast, to link beauty and murder is to create an impasse, a no-way-out situation; it is to stimulate the desire to destroy the world, to "finish it off." So Anne Magnien is right, the advertorial sweeps aside the last taboos, but in the manner of the "new terrorism" that targets museums, churches, historic monuments for attack (in Italy, Switzerland, Turkey) and that massacres tourists, intellectuals, journalists, and passersby. . . .

Succeeding the old "multiples" of Andy Warhol and company, data power's reduction ratio has become the new object of the counterculture. Elizabeth Sussman, chief curator of the Biennale at the Whitney Museum of American Art in New York, chimes in with advertisers, declaring in the spring of 1993, "We need to redefine the art world *in more realistic terms.*" Among the various "lessons in contextualization" offered by her exhibition, one was thus invited to view yet again, for the umpteenth time, the famous video of Rodney King being beaten up, only this time presented and signed with the name of the "auteur," one George Hollyday, the video amateur who witnessed the police violence and also, indirectly, caused the riots, murder, and looting in Los Angeles in April 1992.

From the optical illusion of the cinema motor (the truth twenty-four times a second!) to the final resolution of human clairvoyance through the absolute speed of electromagnetic waves, technical mediatization has progressively revived the techniques of primitive mediatization; attempting to confiscate our immediate rights, without overt violence, it endlessly aggravates the casting aside that excommunication used to accomplish, plunging the greatest number into a now socially untenable *reality effect* with all the resultant geopolitical chaos.

Make no mistake: the *freedom of the media* (democratic rights, the legitimate freedom to inform, to communicate, to circulate) can no longer be separated from the media's liberating power (reduction, proliferation, acceleration, use of communication weapons), from the formation of a frightening mix of *legitimate right* and *established fact.*

THE DATA COUP D'ÉTAT

Speak while you remain silent,
remain silent while you speak.

PROVERB

SINCE MOVEMENT CREATES THE EVENT, the
real is *kinedramatic*. The communications industry would
never have got where it is today had it not started out as an
art of the motor capable of orchestrating the perpetual
shift of appearances.[1]

It has been doing this ever since a record in manufactur-
ing and distribution was attained in 1814, when John Walter II, the owner-editor of the *Times* in London, installed
the first really effective steam press with a capacity of a
thousand pages an hour. This was soon replaced in 1827
with the Cowper and Applegarth press, which could print
five thousand pages an hour on both sides. The first rotary
press was in action in 1848, followed ten years later by a
machine that could run off twenty thousand pages an hour.
At the end of the century, composition also got faster,
thanks to Ottmar Mergenthaler's invention of the linotype.

We might also remember that the *Times* gained another three hours on its competitors by sending papers directly to the country by rail from Euston Station. Great Britain's press amounted to 250 million franked copies a year around 1810; ten years later, the figure was 300 million.[2]

After the shipwrecks and derailments of maritime and rail acceleration, the collisions and crashes of the car and the plane and the steam press, and then the rotary press and the rotary image press of cinematic illusion, wave trains would come along and produce their own specific catastrophes through radio and video signals. News is dynamite, information explodes like a bomb, opinion polls or war propaganda are time bombs, we even have epidemics, for, as lawyer Gisèle Halimi recently wrote, "Nothing is more contagious than the processes of liberation."

Lord Beaverbrook, the grand patron of the British press, was also director of military aeronautics in 1940. His motto: "Wherever I find things organized, I disorganize them."

Already under the Second Empire, Pascal Grousset, editor of *La Marseillaise,* compared his successful rag to "a torpedo boat launched full-speed at the armor-plating of the imperial ship." A little while later, among the organs of the popular press busily abusing republican liberties to make money out of the economic crisis as well as out of scandal and the pillorying of legal entities, publications such as *Le Père Peinard* and *L'En Dehors* went as far as providing readers tempted by anarchy and crime with recipes for explosive cocktails, and even blithely suggested targets. Completely conscious of the reciprocal relationship between events and the press, the anarchists then invented "politics in action." One such anarchist, Jules Bonnot, a great innovator in the crime line, took to thumbing his nose at the heads of the Paris criminal investigation department through the intercession of the press.

During the siege of the building where he was to meet his doom on April 28, 1912, Bonnot wrote, "I am famous. Renown trumpets my name to the four corners of the globe. Enough to make those who go to great lengths to get themselves talked about green with envy." Similarly, on the eve of the Great War, the entire bellicose press would incite patriots to assassinate Jean Jaurès—which was duly carried out on July 31, 1914. Nearly a century later, TV presenter and former legionnaire Charles Villeneuve could still compare TV channel TF1 to "a nuclear aircraft carrier equipped with a tactical nuclear weapon: the Tele-Vision Show."(!) No doubt about it, *only the vectors* change with time. "Eliminating distance kills," René Char once said. When you endlessly increase the liberating power of the media, you bring what was once hidden by distance and the secret—which was distant and naturally foreign to each one of us—far too close; you then run the risk of reinventing, here and now, some kind of *barbarism* (*barbaros* = foreigner, one who does not speak the language). In other words, you run the risk of *inventing the enemy.*

Since *the minds of armed men always waver,* the ancient Greeks accorded the benefit of a certain blindness to bards whose itinerant song was supposed to keep them informed about the appearances of a world where what happens— the surprise, the accident, the eruption of the unforeseen, all that cannot be immediately perceived in the invisible movement of time, *that escapes even the gaze of old men who have seen several generations come and go*—gets mixed up with the ubiquitous tyranny of those rumor-mongers, the vindictive gods, who stir up hatred and unhealthy dreams and lurk in all things though nothing is known of them except by hearsay. . . . [3]

A few millennia later, one realizes that our own era, impious as it may be, has never stopped tarting up the power of its communication tools with the menacing attributes of a theocracy, and that the miraculous credibility of the media, now under a cloud, was perhaps nothing more than one of the last avatars of a once superhuman infallibility. At the beginning of the nineteenth century, the major American newspapers were still able to present themselves not merely as sources of information but as "the gospel truth" and as censors in the social, economic, and political realms. The *New York Tribune* (two hundred thousand copies a day in 1860) was nicknamed "The Great Moral Organ." F. Luther Mott ranked it second *only to the Bible!*

From time immemorial, the "gods" have always been cast as vectors: thus the Egyptians usually translated the name of the god Thoth (who invented language and writing) as Hermes. Hermes then becomes the mediator whose job it is to convey messages and negotiate changes and transitions, but also, equally, to guide, mislead, redirect, and lead astray (a tradition maintained by numerous incarnations of the volatile and polymorphous Greco-Roman Hermes-Mercury). Implicated in the "secret of the gods," the first media thereby invested in hermeticism. Written correspondence that gets in before the event by overcoming distance could effectively look like the "it had to happen" of the *fatum*. In a passage in *The Iliad*, Proitos sends Bellerophontes to Lycia in order to do away with him, entrusting him with "signs of disastrous meaning, many lethal marks that he wrote in a folded tablet, and told him to show them to his father-in-law, to ensure his death." Cryptograms reserved for a small circle of initiates who could communicate regardless of distance, riddles, semantic signals carved into a tree, a rock, designating a rendezvous, marking a route, awaiting a stray nomad.

When the use of language or writing spreads and comes to guarantee democratic laws, an antidote immediately appears in the form of new epistolary codes. Plutarch cites the Spartans' secret methods of correspondence. But cryptography, strictly speaking, in the sense of the substitution of numbers, words, or symbols, was of Semitic origin. The prophet Jeremiah is said to have been among the first to use a cryptographic system, well before reigning powers like the deified caesars used permutations in simple applications.

From the message's secret as appropriation of the divine *fatum*, things took certain decisive turns: the military regimes of ancient Greece, such as Sparta's timarchy, were based on an arithmetical division of goods (spoils) and a geometric division of space (colonization). The change in the scale of war with the end of local combat and the emergence of the great Hellenic states would require an essential division of information and would soon lead to a *theory of mediatization.*

In one generation, Herodotus's *history (historia),* which still held to the Homeric tradition, gave way to the *superjournalism* of Thucydides, recounting the wars he took part in. Brushing aside the enigma of divine intervention, Thucydides focuses on eyewitness accounts, ensuring their exactness by a system of information cross-checking combined with serious critical analysis.

The history of Greece, however, preserves a strong emotional charge in which the military necessity for democratic cohesion makes itself felt.

You cannot effectively improvise a citizen any more than you can become a killer on your own. There must be common rituals, a certain trancelike state, for one to manage to leave one's body, to become one's own double, to pass from one's own *identity* to *identification* with some *warrior who has already died in the City.*

Because it is easier to fool a crowd than it is to fool a single person, the forming of *public opinion* in Greece is associated with the military trance. Public opinion, Plato tells us, will be "an *intermediate state* between knowledge and ignorance, touching on the vast majority of things." He adds that "the visible world is the domain of opinion." Socrates will be anxious about the education of Greek children—an education based on Homer's epics and the songs of the bards, with their quota of crime, incest, violence, hate, revenge, and family atrocities and having no cathartic effect whatsoever as far as he is concerned (quite the opposite—no more, anyway, than the tragic theater that comes after). *Able to move everyone on the spot,* the minstrels of tragedy wander from city to city, bringing the multitudes together in theaters like the one at Epidaurus, which already held fourteen to fifteen thousand seats. There, what is declaimed, sung, imagined, attacked, becomes *the domain of the visible* for all present. The secret, the intimate, personal truth are now considered a break with mass communication, all democratic truths having now to be found in common, to become collective, through theater, just as in the assembly or court of law. Plato makes an objective statement about this: *You can easily imitate appearances, but not reality.* Just as a magician can quickly, very quickly even, "*make* the sun and the stars in the heavens, the earth, himself, and other animals and plants." It's all done with mirrors.

What we have on the ancient theater stage is already actual *plagiarism of the visible world.* The first mass media, designed to crack open the secret and educate public opinion, are just a trick effect of reality, a mise-en-scène with changing sets, disguises, machinery, and *dei ex machina.* In the *Republic,* Plato also notes that democracy certainly has its "charms"; it is, he says, "a veritable hodgepodge of constitutions," a shopwindow in which the whole heterogeneous kit and caboodle of optical illusions lie piled up "like one of those many-colored garments that women and children just adore." *But,* the philosopher asks in conclusion, *are there any states of existence that are not perverse?*

On the battlefield, the disciplinary logistics of the new democratic armies are also supposed to pull off this excessive incorporation of parts into a whole capable of a common movement, are they not? Suggestions and hallucinations mushroom, war machines multiply, fiercely blazing mirrors induce blindness or fire, and when "glorious Hector reaches out to take his son . . . , the child shrank back crying against the breast of his girdled nurse, terrified at the sight of his own father, frightened by the bronze and the crest of horse-hair, as he saw it nodding grimly down at him from the top of his father's helmut" *(The Iliad, VI).*

In Greek antiquity, whenever democracy pits itself against the tyranny of a small or single group, the democrats always claim to be replacing brute physical force with a moral force allowed by a mass mediatization that flies in the face of the very concept of reality. So it is only natural that in the city-states where this kind of cinetheatrics are big, certain faux philosophers and sophists begin to develop increasingly perverse techniques of persuasion from the fourth century B.C. on: that *ancient eloquence* that was so little concerned with what was true or false regardless of the issue, happy just to hurry events along and offer information about the instability of the world.

Sophists such as Plato's Thrasymachus, who chased young men and diverse profits, was a false rhetorician and occasional informer and yet excelled in "whipping up the

crowds and then calming them down again *as if by magic.*"
For Lucian, eloquence is like theater or the tribunal; it is "a
battle against the inertia of images *that one could make
people see but that would have no movement or signs of
life.*" Seneca thought the fact of being compressed into a
verse or saying gives thought *the force of a projectile hurled
by some vigorous arm.* Eloquence is less a means of communicating than a communication weapon in which the
energy of delivering information is often combined with
that of denunciation, of attack. No one knew better than
Thrasymachus how to hurl or refute an accusation, Plato
again notes. Archaeological sites are littered with vestiges
of such democratic eloquence—with *ostrakons,* the remains of vast numbers of votes that often called for irrevo-
cable decisions, potshards, carved shells on which the kinedramatic destiny of the *polis* was written, day by day, along
with the necessity, for each and every person, *of being
wherever the others are,* at the same point in space: the
agora, theater, stadium, or assembly. . . . Ostracism has often been called *"the reverse vote"* and is certainly a carry-
over from athymie and primitive stoning, collective murder. But we might also wonder if the old tyranny was now
appropriate to the endlessly expanding city, to urban chaos
in general, whether it was able to maintain its effectiveness
there. At the "policing" level, mass communication was effective in other ways once it became a system of general in-
crimination.

A bit like *politically correct* language, that so-called *(cul-
turally sensitive)* verbal rigor from which American democ-

racy is now suffering and which reeks of lynching, "in this moribund system that leads to anarchy while claiming to resist the reduction of the many to the few" (Emerson), antiquity's denunciatory eloquence was not aimed at punishing crimes or attacks on the *polis*. It was aimed at outstripping these, at getting a jump on crime thanks to an obsessional vigilance in the form of a *permanent statistical opinion poll*.

Ostracizing a group or a person means "turfing out" an undesirable, one who through ambition, personal genius, or services rendered becomes too "heavy" and so risks putting a spanner in the works of the democratic machine, in the manner of Hercules, excluded from the argonauts' ship because he weighed too much and might have caused the ship to come to grief.

In the United States in 1890, the results of a census were analyzed by means of punch cards, a process that already allowed faster and more sophisticated statistical evaluation. In the French elections of 1992, a hundred years later, the role of *televised polls* was more impressive than ever. There was even a plan to keep broadcasting poll results right up to the last minute under the pretext of *democratizing information,* though this would have been illegal. René Rémond, among others, actually spoke of election polls as a *"first round."*

As another stab at a future *cathodic democracy,* in certain constituencies the smart card, designed to count votes electronically and thus speed up the publication of results, was tried out for the first time.

Each new regime remains unrecognizable when it emerges since it preserves certain traits of the preceding regime, much as a son looks vaguely like his father. We have thus, without realizing it, gone from simple statistical management to a new phenomenon of *representation,* the virtual theatricalization of the real world.

We had to wait for the fusion/confusion of information and data processing to obtain the fusion/confusion of *the secret of speed*—initially, with the first military decoders to become operational during the Second World War. These ancestors of our computers and software systems were also heirs to the obsessional vigilance and providence of ancient democracies. . . . After this, with real-time transmission and transcription of the message or image, we would be tempted to compensate for any erratic behavior on the part of the public and to finally achieve higher *success rates* (the power to correctly predict) than what the classic methods of statistics allow in the areas of economics, military action, industry, and, eventually, even politics.

If the destiny of the city-state depended on each person's obligation to be where the others were, then for the victims of multiple solitude, the televised poll is now a mere pale simulation of the ancient rallying of citizens, of their movement to the urns and the final result.

As we have seen, the gap between the speed of prognosis and the slowness of the actual political act is endlessly narrowing, already causing some to confuse the latter with the premature displaying of results on the television screen. After *war games* and other reflex games, they may as well le-

galize *binary political simulators,* the electronic home vote
that could act instantaneously, a "hodgepodge of constitutions" now turned into a *cathodic shopwindow display:
democratic software* whose "politically correct" programs
only a handful of initiated informers would control. The
principle of this new interactive game has been on the
drawing board for a long time. American president Rich-
ard Nixon gave it his enthusiastic support back in the early
1970s.

Tennyson claimed that, along with a touch of anarchy,
democracies bear within them the seeds of their own doom
and the probability of a return to tyranny. Similarly, the anarchic carving-up of representational techniques, in provoking the implosion of the visible world, which was once
the domain of public opinion, inexorably catapults us into
this final phase of political *mediatization*—which becomes,
once more, the privilege of smaller and smaller groups,
keepers of that ultimate strange brew composed of the
speed of light (the secret) and the exorbitant eloquence of
figures, messages, and images (information).

THE SHRINKING
EFFECT

Living means being blind to one's own dimensions.

CIORAN

WITH ACCELERATION THERE IS NO more here
and there, only the mental confusion of near and far, present and future, real and unreal—a mix of history, stories,
and the hallucinatory utopia of communication technologies. This usurpation by information has crept up over
the years disguised in the glad rags of ideologies of progress, stripped of all judgment, and giving Merleau-Ponty
pause for thought at the end of his life: "Since the same
words—idea, freedom, knowledge—cannot have the same
meaning in different places unless we were to have a single
witness reducing them to some common denominator, how
can we hope to see a single philosophy grow out of the various philosophies?" Though not able to occupy the same
place and time by means of the optical illusion of cinema's
sights, nineteenth-century folk could at least hope to share,

shortly, the *same time,* relying on the excess speed of broadcasting and communications technology. "Cultural evolution is like an army on the march. . . . I may well be living in 1913, but one of my neighbors is living in 1900, the other in 1880. The peasant of the upper Tyrol is stuck in the seventh century. . . . How lucky countries like America are not to have stragglers and marauders!"[1]

For Adolf Loos, as for Darwin, busily elaborating his theory of evolution as he sailed around the world in the *Beagle,* the greater the distance between here and there, the more the native appears to be living in times long gone, in prehistoric times, spared the movement of progress.

If this spatiotemporal perspective is abolished by the acceleration effects of communication technologies, then all of Earth's inhabitants may well wind up thinking of themselves more as *contemporaries* than as *citizens;* they may in the process slip out of the contiguous space, distributed by quota, of the old Nation-State (or City-State), which harbored the *demos,* and into the atopic community of a "Planet-State."

An early sign of this new breed of data coup, the first gazettes (from the Italian *gazetta* = small change) were called *courants* (currents) in France. A complex term, stemming from the Latin *currere,* this indicates at once rapidity of movement in space from here to there, and *what is currently occurring in time* and which is not yet over at the time of writing or reading. Before becoming a periodical, the *courant* was, in fact, a diary or a report of important meetings or long-distance voyages, a ship's log.

Similarly, gazettes were also simple letters, private chronicles reserved for a select number of readers. With their rumors and supply of gossip and news, they involved an art of writing that broke with the techniques and rules of classical literature in the middle of the eighteenth century. Madame de Sévigné referred to her letters as gazettes, justifying Marcel Proust's reflection that "the Marquise does not present things in their logical, causal order."

Under Louis XV, the gutted galleries of the cloître des Cordeliers sheltered newswriters who both *listened* and *read*. The press effectively came into being in France, in those public places where *stock exchanges* known as *squads* were set up to allow written or oral information to be exchanged. These were distant prototypes of the future large-scale international agencies such as Havas, which formed in 1830, followed by Reuters in London, Wolf in Berlin, and Associated Press in New York.

Worldly political newswriters frequented salons and literary and philosophical circles, political cafés like the Procope, the promenades, the Tuileries, the Feuillants, the shopping arcades of the Palais-Royal—all the general headquarters of cosmopolitanism, prostitution, gambling, and police informing.

In June 1789, Arthur Young registered his amazement at the number of illegal pamphlets that appeared in Paris daily, as well as at the general ebullience reigning precisely at the Palais-Royal, centered on certain zealous orators. A little later, Article XI of the Declaration of the Rights of Man and the Citizen granted total liberty to a press that

was specifically used, according to Young, for the propaga-
tion of seditious ideas, calumny, and fabricated news.

Three hundred such publications sprang up overnight,
mostly in Paris; for the very first time the population was
subject to daily incitement by an *information tool.*

Public leaflets would thus take their place among "the
many theatrical ventures with which the vivid imagination
of the French revolutionaries embellished the tale of their
struggle for liberty."[2] *It is easier to fool a crowd than a single person.* There was no point in being able to read: town
criers and newspaper hawkers, spreading out along the
streets of the capital, sang out headlines and startling news,
stirring up the population, getting in ahead of the event,
sowing panic and provoking massacre and riot. This ten-
dentious press was three days ahead of the arrest and exe-
cution of Robespierre and his cohorts, succeeding in getting a jump on them perhaps because the Incorruptible still
believed that *history was the past loaded with an at-present*
as in the City of antiquity. But history was already completely turned toward the future, whisked along by the liberating power of the new media.

Victor Hugo would later note in *Acts and Words* (1875)
that "all histories are the story of the past. The history of
the Revolution is the story of the future. The Revolution
conquered in advance. . . . There is more of the promised
land than territory gained in what it brought us; if any of
these advance conquests ever enters the human realm, a
fresh aspect of the Revolution will be revealed." The revolution that conquers in advance, this totality that gets pur-

sued yet escapes once more, the *promised land*—all so
many hollow phrases unless applied to the technological
revolution that would inaugurate a new, parallel apperception of space and time within the history of the representation of history.

After centuries of the monarchy, the first republic springs
up *in three days* out of a news event: the announcement of
the victory of Valmy on September 20, 1792 and the arrest
of the Prussian invasion. On the twenty-first, the Convention declares the abolition of royalty and on the twenty-
second, decides that all public acts from now on will be
dated from the Year I of the Republic of France.

Unlike previous republics in history, this republic was
born not of sedition, but of the instant implementation of a
form of mediatization with totalitarian ambitions, as well
as of the establishment of an irrefutable technical fact, as
opposed to some legitimate state that would then become
dependent on the technology. A few months before the new
regime was proclaimed, the physicist Claude Chappe had
presented his optical telegraph project to the legislative assembly as "a reliable means of setting up a correspondence
in such a way that the legislative body could send its orders
to the front and receive a reply *in a single sitting.*"

Equally significantly, Chappe saw the telegraph as a way
of harnessing an inexperienced press whose area of operations was still fairly tiny, as Young had remarked, barely
extending beyond the Paris Commune. Chappe writes to
Lakanal, "The best response to journalists who think
France is too spread out to form a republic is to install the

telegraph. The telegraph shrinks distances and in a way joins an entire, huge population *into a single point.*"[3]

Perhaps not the geographical point of the agora of antiquity anymore, but already *the same point in time—or as good as.* . . . Barère, who dreamed of transforming French soil into "one vast camp," announces, on August 17, 1794, the transmission by telegraph of the news of the taking of Quesnoy: "With this invention," he tells the Assembly, "*distance between places vanishes.*"

The telescoping of near and far had indeed brought about marked progress since the beginning of the eighteenth century, such as "surveillance of the heavens" with the construction of national observatories, Halley's idea of an "astronomic unit," and the manned flight in 1793 of the Montgolfière, a hot-air balloon that would pass the 11,000-meters altitude mark the following century.

The ambition then of most balloonists was not so much *to fly* as *to see from on high,* like Lucian's Icaromenippus, who was not satisfied just to chart his course by the stars, but began traveling among them, "climbing as far as the moon" so that he could see Earth as a small thing, much smaller than the moon seen from Earth![4]

In his book *Paintings,* August Wilhelm Schlegel, a contemporary of the hot-air balloon, imagines three young art lovers contemplating the Elbe valley: " 'All landscape painting is a sort of miniature,' the sculptor Waller said to his friend Rheinhold. 'To get a huge vista or towering mountain down on canvas, how we have to compress them!' " Rheinhold immediately retorts, " '*They compress themselves!*' "

Rheinhold shows Waller the right approach: first you deliberately abstract yourself from the incommensurable grandeur of the landscape, which goes beyond our angle of vision wherever we look and *forces us to take in the measure of our smallness.* " 'You need only look into the distance through a narrow window or between your cupped hands to see how many large objects your eyes can take in. . . . The eye can only grasp the apparent magnitude of things in their converse relationships.' "

He gleefully goes on to invoke the aerial perspective or "bird's-eye" view, a most fashionable mode of representation in the eighteenth century. " 'This has the amazing power of representing size on a grand scale over a small area. One might even imagine the bird's-eye view taking on the colossal!' " At one extreme of a cartography whose scale would be visual illusion, the painting would become an *outsize miniature.*

Since we never stop thinking in dimensions, we cannot possibly see, and since space and time are merely something we intuit, tools of apperception and communication finally manage to pull off that *paradox of appearances* whereby the greatness of the universe is compressed in a perpetual *shrinking effect.*

Cioran once said, "Living means being blind to one's own dimensions." Like the landscape that stretches unobstructed at the feet of Rheinhold and company as far as the

eye can see, the historic past that endlessly reduces us
to scorn for our smallness can also be compressed. Similarly, the great precipitation Hugo noted, the "advance
conquest" of an excessive revolution, could play itself out
over the entire territory of France in a few hours, in a few
minutes, in a single session of the Assembly. Through such
illusory technical mastery of a *totality that can shrink,* the
acceleration of history becomes observable. As for counter-
revolutionaries, who are either forgotten or executed,
Robespierre and his cronies will regard them as "a few
small human figures," as though already viewing them
from afar, barely able to make them out. We can also ap-
preciate the immediate usefulness of the Year I of a republican calendar that, in the name of rationalism, claims to
make a clean sweep of the historic past and above all to
abolish religion's *long haul,* established according to bibli-
cal chronology in which the unit of time is the millennium.[5]
The French revolutionaries were thereby getting stuck into
a certain Judeo-Christian practice. But, well beyond this,
they were also trying to reconcile history's acceleration
with the brevity of human life, taking as their model a scientific method that at the time was still limited to observation depending on pretty poor means of perception and
verification, often restricted to a few decades and consequently subject to hasty conclusions. Like official science,
the pseudosciences and philosophies of history could
promptly sally forth into the impasse of positivism's short-
term certitudes. In his report of August 1794, Lakanal
claimed that the optical telegraph was a speedy harbinger

of thought *rivaling thought in speed*. Feeling itself under threat, the nascent press took up the challenge launched by a communications system primarily of interest to the army, to politicians, and to the state police. The press would reveal imagination to be *excess thought speed* able to overcome the relative slowness of cottage industry transmission technology and eternally ahead of the event. "The press is not today, it is yesterday!" as Gaston Leroux would say. In *1915*, Karl Kraus asked, "How is the world ruled and led to war? Diplomats lie to journalists, then believe what they've said when they see it in print." *The thing described takes over from the real thing.* Before achieving this effective power, however, the press first had to come up with a *parallel information market* in which, according to Maupassant, *realism is an illusion.*

So what happens in the nineteenth century is a process whereby industrial concerns come together, with the press then quietly gaining a hold over them. The optical and electrical telegraph partly eluded state monopoly and caused commercial sea and rail trade to double before entering the public domain. An electrical telegraph became operational at the Central Post Office in London in 1850 and in France in 1856. At the same time, kiosks and bookshops sprang up at railway stations. The combination targeted a growing urban public more and more in a hurry: data transmission, the conveyance of travelers and goods for sale, and, finally, the very latest innovation designed to fill the gaps in long-distance communication and to develop the script of what might end up turning into

some kind of *virtual reality*, the *literary chronicle*, the serial. The *feuilleton* first crops up in France in 1800 in *Le
Journal des débats*. Neither a novel nor a political tract,
this is already a substratum of daily life, with its *faits
divers*, ads, art and theater reviews, recipes, and tales of
travel. When Girardin manages to win over traditionally
hostile French men of letters to the popular press, the former have merely to delve into the social breeding ground
of the *feuilleton* for instant inspiration, producing new
schools such as realism and naturalism, not to mention
the detective novel or "literature for ocean crossings."[6]

Stendhal, who was a journalist in England, thought of
the novel as a mirror dragged along a highway. Dickens directly applied the rules of a hard-pressed press to his literary works. As a young journalist, he was sent to the country to file daily reports on election campaigns for the
Morning Chronicle. At night, by the dim light of a lantern,
he would transcribe his text from a post-chaise and four,
galloping along at full pelt, and hand over each sequence of
copy as soon as it was finished to dispatch riders on horse-
back stationed at carefully chosen spots along the way,
who would then deliver the material to the printer. Dickens
submitted to this same rhythm all his life, the pace of serial-
ization of his novels scarcely leaving him a fortnight ahead
of his distributors every month.[7]

He tells the story of one day seeing a reader ask for the
monthly update—"the new green number"—of *David
Copperfield* (1849). When the shop assistant hands her the
installment, she glances at it and says, "Oh, this I have

read. I want the next one." Dickens concludes, "Listening to this, unrecognized, and remembering that not one word of the number she was asking for was yet written, for the first and only time in my life, I felt—frightened."

The acceleration of information drove it to its own deregulation. The imaginary relayed the reality of the facts, while journalists and admen gave themselves over to the perilous game of prognostics. In 1927, the French press accordingly lay bets on the east-west crossing of the North Atlantic by Nungesser and Coli in their airplane, the *White Bird*. All the papers gave detailed accounts of the two aviators' triumphant arrival in New York, the joy of victor and delirious crowd alike, the historic speeches pronounced on the occasion. . . . At the very moment that these reports were sending figures for the leading dailies soaring, the heroes of the day were already lost with all hands somewhere off the American coast they were never to reach. But editors and journalists were able to get themselves out of hot water by accusing the government and ministers concerned of having primed them with false information. What is truly remarkable is that the public blamed the Republican government and let the press off practically scot-free.

In fact, subscribers had long ago made the connection between the illusion of long-distance information, the virtuality of the serial novel, and the excitement of the gambling games the leading dailies ran—raffles, lotteries, competitions—not to mention stock exchange reports, horoscopes, and all the major racing events—rallies, horse races and records, foot races, car races, air races, boat races, bike races. On a loftier plane, the international press would organize dangerous, far-off expeditions to add a little spice to peacetime, so the most blasé readers could lay a few pennies or cents (the price of their paper) on the success of adventures as mythical as the conquest of the North Pole (1909), the scaling of Mount Everest, or the chances of explorer Henry Morton Stanley's finding Livingstone in Africa as he was engaged to do by the *New York Herald* in 1871.

All the famous novelists or writers were, at some time or other, chroniclers, reviewers, or war correspondents.[8] The press would thus exercise near-absolute control over the book industry; it would also have "an influence on the arts and letters and on thought that no prince, no judge, no patron or censor had ever dared claim till then," as Louis Veuillot was to write, asserting that reviews would end up doing the book in. But it was not reviews or rigged literary prizes that would kill the book; "literature for ocean crossings" ran out of steam at the same time geographical distances did, thanks to the shrinking effect produced by the acceleration of transmission and transport technologies.

Hugo spoke to journalists of "things seen"; a few decades later, Cendrars imagines "word photographs," and, in 1928, Mac Orlan announces in *Les Annales,* "In twenty-five years, all writer-reporters will be able to wield a camera." No need to be a man of letters to wield a camera-pen. Novelist-reporters would be quickly mown down as journalists themselves turned to literature. *Le Petit Parisien*'s literary critic, Henri Beraud, one of Albert Londres's pals, received the Goncourt in 1922. At Albin Michel, he founded the "Grands Reportages" series, covering all the big stories and instituting *bookshop journalism.*

The first routing of the written word was brought about by two crucial events. In the 1920s, newsreels had become a staple feature of the normal picture-theater program. But any reality-based cinema would always be paralyzed by the long delay required to get films produced and distributed. This *loss of speed* further promoted the print media, which would remain *first with the news* right up until the WIRE-LESS, initially reserved for military purposes, joined the ranks of the mass media. In 1924, the antenna on top of the Eiffel Tower was "demilitarized" and a journalist named Maurice Privat installed a small radio studio on the north pylon. The first SPOKEN NEWS was broadcast on November 3, 1925. It began every evening at six o'clock and was followed by a music program at nine. This was also the beginning of the publicity slot and even the first forms of home shopping.

In the United States, five years previously to the day, Westinghouse had opened the first authorized commercial radio station, KDKA. The first program that went to air was political, essentially giving the results of the Harding versus Cox presidential election. The little station actually owed the results, which it communicated zealously and which were, moreover, unreliable, to the *Pittsburgh Post.* Radio broadcasting would long remain an offshoot of the major newspapers' investment programs and of the powerful infrastructure of the international agencies. But from 1924 on, radio advertising made its appearance on a national scale, and, in 1925, coast-to-coast wireless communication was up and running.

Stations quickly sorted out their political alignments. It was no longer a matter of instructing or simply informing, but of entertaining, amusing, captivating the greatest possible number; for this, they had a specific trump card up their sleeves: the universal language of music, which could revitalize the cinedramatic effect of the written word, especially the novel. Then came that famous day of October 23, 1927, on which American commercial cinema entered a new era with the beginning of the talkies and the triumph of *The Jazz Singer,* the film that tells the story of a white man, son of a religious Jewish cantor, who dons blackface in order to transform himself into a black jazz artist. The ambiguity of the scenario, with its switch of roles, ethnicities, and cultures, the almost total absence of dialogue, already heralded the United States's powerful *musical logistics*—that quasi-military conditioning music allows with its rhythmic codes regressing to the classic scales of archaic music, associated with notions of distance, timbre, and echo.

With the onset of the Great Depression of the 1930s, the advertising revenue of the press suddenly plummeted, whereas wireless revenue continued to climb. So the major newspapers declared war on radio, and press agencies opted to stop selling them information, which meant radio stations then had to gather it themselves. This was a serious misreading of the liberating power of communication technologies. After many a setback, radio news soon asserted its supremacy—with a little help from the tragic events then overturning Europe. On March 12, 1938, the first multiplex broadcast in history went to air. Correspondents that CBS had posted in Rome, Berlin, and Paris could deliver their impressions instantaneously over the twenty-day Munich *Putsch*. The intensivity of this news was definitely beyond the print media.

The old adage that *information is almost the only product that is worthless the next day* thus needs careful reconsideration. In the nineteenth century and the beginning of the twentieth, when the press was in its heyday, the issue, as we have seen, was not so much "making news" as getting in before it, while it was happening, so as to finally sell it before it was literally overtaken, passé. Subscribers were not so much buying daily news as they were buying instantaneity, ubiquity—in other words, their own participation in universal contemporaneity, in the movement of the future Planet City.

The unscrupulous Bunau Varilla, who took over *Le Matin* in 1896, got it right when he saw a perfect accord between the logic of commerce and the speed of media conveyance and transmission. He circled the paper's title with a double telegraphic score, adding below the inscription, "The modern music of rapid knowledge with the only French newspaper to link the four major capitals of the world by special cable." A confirmed technophile, Varilla treated his staff, on the other hand, with contempt. *Le*

Matin journalists and correspondents were mere faceless employees and had to remain anonymous. When Varilla finally let them sign their articles, it was not with their actual names but with the names of railway stations.

Another anecdote related by Stéphane Lauzanne in *Sa Majesté la Presse* (1925) shows how far the liberating power of the media had stolen a march on information content from the nineteenth century onward: "A Berlin correspondent for the *Times* made the grave mistake of hopping on a train to personally deliver to his chief editor in London a news item of vital interest:

" 'You can publish it tonight in the *Latest Intelligence* and date it from Berlin!'

" 'No, that's impossible!'

" 'What do you mean impossible?'

" 'It's impossible because it's not the latest, since it's still only four o'clock in the afternoon and it's not from Berlin, since you're here.' The famous Delane added, 'Unless you take the next train back to Berlin and wire your piece to me from there. I will never offer an article from London as a dispatch from Berlin!' " The technical difficulty was finally overcome and the article was published, not in the *Latest Intelligence,* but before this, with the uncompromising note, "from our Berlin correspondent, currently in London." Doubt about how far away the emission was broadcast remained and subscribers got their money's worth!

"The press had to prove it could bring down one regime and put together another in the middle of a revolution," writes Charles Ledré on the events of 1830 in Paris. History shows that ever since their technical liberation, the industrial media have never stopped bringing down regimes or selling them out as soon as they have set them up. In the eighteenth century, already rearing to sink the divine-right monarchy, they betrayed the Republic for the Directoire and the Directoire for the Empire. Thanks to the fact that the opposition press was playing the same game, they supported the Restoration against the Empire as soon as they could, then the Republic against royalty. . . . And now they are tearing into consultative democracy in the United States, France, Japan, et cetera. One could find plenty of economic reasons for the way this paraconstitutional power has acted. Media trusts, since the nineteenth century, have often been in the hands of political movers closely connected to financial and diplomatic circles, from Emile de Girardin to Loucheur, Pierre Laval, Hennessy, Robert Hersant. The political ambitions of the media are nothing new.

In the nineteenth century, the large-scale press already tried to convert its *subscribers* into *voters*. Certain newspaper barons, such as Henry Debergue, even proposed to do away with the political class by making elections a game of chance, suggesting a sort of *electoral raffle* be set up, with deputies being drawn at random from among ordinary citizens the way juries are; the results were to be published in the dailies much as the day's trading on the stock market.

Apropos Elie Joseph Bois, a shyster on the take and on close terms with the Quai d'Orsay who ran *Le Petit Parisien* for nearly thirty years (one and a half million copies a day), Louise Weiss points to the "formidable electoral potential of Bois's paper, which places him above all suspicion." Pierre Assouline notes that over the same period, a paragraph or column that a journalist might devote to some speech delivered in the House would lend it a *legitimacy* it otherwise would not have.

Whenever there is mention of such editorials—thought of as an *antechamber to Parliament* well before television would add its stock of representatives and senators—the idea keeps returning that information somehow has a *legitimacy* that gives it a different kind of power from that of democratic legitimacy: the power of an ever-present, de facto usurpation.

In the middle of the Gulf War, Françoise Giroud thus remarked in *Le Nouvel Observateur,* "The Prime Minister officially put on guard anyone who might be tempted to exploit public sentiment (regarding Saddam Hussein's hostages). But he does not have the power to coerce, which is just as well. Between two evils we must never choose censorship. It's up to the heads of the television channels to show proof of judgment." This is an incredibly blatant argument, for it attributes to television heads a discretionary power it denies the heads of an elected government. Better still, it implies that only government censorship is unacceptable and that the censorship exercised by TV chiefs is as perfectly legitimate as it is legal.

But if we just cast our minds back to that maelstrom of information in which everything changes, is exchanged, opens up, collapses, fades away, gets buried, gets resurrected, flourishes, and finally evaporates in the course of a day—and after a while much less than this, in the very instant, we might say, that it surges up in real time, twenty-four hours a day—it then becomes clear that duration is the media's natural enemy the way water is fire's. If a *conservative* press were not a contradiction in terms, it would be a pure aberration from a news point of view.

Speed guarantees the *secret* and thus the *value* of all information. Liberating the media therefore means not only annihilating the duration of information—of the image and its path—but with these all that endures or persists. What the mass media attack in other institutions (democracy, justice, science, the arts, religion, morality, culture) is not the institutions themselves but the instinct of self-preservation that lies behind them. That is, what they still retain of bygone civilizations for whom everything was a material and spiritual preparation directed against disappearance and death, and in which communicating meant to survive, to remain.

In 1915, at the start of the First World War, "deserter journalist" Karl Kraus denounced "the abominable amalgam of a certain emotional life and an everyday object, the press, which whole populations take on trust with all its noxious cant.

"They bombard the soul with all this stuff. And in between war reports, they take up 'The Battle against Censorship' and declare war with 'The Campaign against Borrowing' and even 'The War against Conscription.' It's true that journalists, businessmen, and pacifists have talked like soldiers all their lives. Well let them stick to their guns, if they want to talk like soldiers. Soldiers, though, should talk differently, and not like journalists talking like soldiers, but like soldiers. *Though it is probably impossible to tell the difference.*"[9]

Originating in civil and international war as well as in army logistics, the modern information complex cunningly preserves the deadly features of these. "We ought to acknowledge the significance for mankind of the simultaneous invention of gunpowder and printer's ink," says Karl Kraus, further. We might add that a similar connection exists between, say, the machine gun and the camera, nitrocellulose and film, radar and video—but also between the *trick effects* of the depiction of actual events in graphic illustration, photography, film, and television and good old military *camouflage,* designed to conceal armaments, convoys, and troop movements from the observer's prying eyes and to leave the enemy in the lurch, no longer able to tell *where reality begins or leaves off.* It is no accident that *L'Excelsior,* the first major French daily to systematically use photographs of real events on the front page, was financed by Bazil Zaharoff, the famous arms dealer who made a fortune in 1914. Also during the war, aware that its war effort was flagging, Germany bought certain organs of the French press under the counter and even tried to buy Havas! At the same time Hollywood and the UFA (Universum-Film-Aktiengesellschaft) enjoyed the support of heavy industry and the transport industry. It seems we

may be forced to agree with Charles I of the Austro-
Hungarian Empire, when he said, just after the war ended,
that *newspapers like a good crime, but they like a good war
even better* and that *without the press, the bloodbath of
1914 would never have occurred.* Or perhaps we might
agree with Bismarck that newspapers were the cause of at
least three wars; he adds, "Sooner or later every country
ends up paying for the windows their press has thrown a
brick through."

We can see this happening again in Lebanon, India, Rus-
sia, Yugoslavia. So much so that in 1993, the European
Commission, backed in particular by Unesco, decided to
defuse the dangerous power of the various media by arm-
ing a radio ship, the *Right to Speak,* with a 50-kilowatt
transmitter with a range of about 200 kilometers. Based off
the Dalmatian Coast in international waters, it has a team
of seven professional journalists on board from Serbia,
Croatia, Slovenia, and Bosnia. Their mission is to bring
pluralist information to the inhabitants of the former fed-
eration as objectively as possible. The *Right to Speak*
broadcasts twenty-four hours a day, alternating news, debate, and music programs. The promoters hope thereby to
tone down the hatred and to counter the bellicose propaganda of the different media by employing "reciprocity of
action," the mutual capacity of the event and the mass media to inform each other, for pacific purposes.[10]

It seems that there are *just wars but not innocent armies.*
International law, however, distinguishes between war

crimes and crimes against humanity, the latter enjoying no amnesty. Information professionals may not always escape judgment and condemnation in critical periods, but, like the military, they often claim lack of responsibility, a certain dose of Freudian innocence, an open, frank relationship with their communication weapons—precision cameras, videos, and broadcasting equipment that only get more and more accurate.

But the similarities do not end there. Apart from having obscure suppliers, the ranks of the mass media, like those of the army, include *francs tireurs* (freelancers)—countless specialized corps and commandos whose heroes die in action—reporters, photographers, filmmakers who suffer and do battle on the ground but who are not above the odd threat or bribe if it means bringing back stories and images they sometimes sign with their own blood. To say nothing of the brass of editorial committees with their strategists and marshals and solemn prize-giving ceremonies such as for the Pulitzer Prize, the Albert-Londres, Sept d'or, and so on. Finally, the propaganda services, the industrial advertising machine that more or less discreetly infiltrates the swing to extremes of opinion campaigns. The media evolve in tandem with the army. Today they do not much look like a republican army, itself in decline; rather, they show signs of a certain military anarchy, their fields of tension gradually eluding any effective control, like the lost regiments, terrorist factions, lone killers looming up here and there around the world, provoking clashes that have become endemic. They used to say *peace lasts longer than war.* This was almost true in the era of nuclear dissuasion, before the new news networks were in place, which no truce, no peace can possibly effect. Subject to the tyranny of real time, the media are no longer now fighting *all that endures,* peace along with the rest. Now it is the media who no longer have any more time, no time to delay. Territorial distance and media proximity make an explosive cocktail. At the end of the 1980s, when Mikhail Gorbachev implemented *glasnost,* before being eliminated with the help of the media he had freed, or when the same media staged Tiananmen Square or triumphantly orchestrated the fall of the Berlin Wall and the overturning of the bronze giants of communism's demigods, it was very much the birth pangs of a data coup d'état that we were witnessing, with the revelation of the absolute incompatibility between old national, political, and economic territories and the contemporaneity of a universal *dromos* that has finally been achieved.

With the telegraph, distances and territorial boundaries evaporate; with real-time technologies, real presence bites the dust. Remember what happened to poor old Olivier Stirn in July 1990. The unfortunate minister for tourism had been asked to organize a conference on progress with the most eminent members of the French Left and the Rocard government. Anxious to fill the room, the minister had the bright idea of recruiting a hundred or so "extras," out-of-work actors registered with the ANPE (Agence nationale pour l'emploi). As though by chance, the media got wind of it and exposed the sham. Parliamentary democracy

was seen for what it has become: exiled from the public
arena and especially from the *demos,* with the prospect of
an empty room and debators addressing thin air. Olivier
Stirn was forced to resign.

In contrast, when President Reagan used to stop at the
top of the gangway of the presidential plane to salute an
absent crowd and a deserted airport under the eye of the
camera, no one was shocked because one rightly imagined
that Reagan's wave could just as well be addressed to home
viewers in their armchairs as to whatever supporters might
be there on the tarmac. While television practices designed
to oust the parliamentary system abound—polls and refer-
endums on "major social issues" through computer-link
systems such as Minitel—to try to prove at any cost, as
Olivier Stirn did, that there still exists a public space peopled by flesh and blood citizens, is to be guilty of a *crime of
lèse-media.*

*The abominable amalgam of a certain emotional life
and an everyday object accepted on trust* is now complete.
Extrapolating from Karl Kraus's remark, we could say the
anarchic proliferation of our handy communication tools
has surreptitiously accustomed us to such a series of dis-
creet disappearances and multiple absences, that it is definitely the real presence of people and the natural correla-
tion between things that now seems disturbing and even
unacceptable to us, forcing us to deny them, to reject our
kith and kin.

Recently mankind's most senior citizen, Jeanne Calment,
was asked what technical feat most astonished her in her

nearly one hundred and twenty years. She answered without hesitation that it was not the movies or the airplane, it was the telephone. One can imagine that of all inventions, the telephone seemed the most startling simply by virtue of being the most *supernatural.* Cinema was an extension of photography and the kaleidoscope, budding aviation of the kite and observation of the flight of birds, whereas hearing the voice of someone alive yet not there, who may be hundreds of kilometers away, being able to rouse them and converse long-distance with them in the absence of their body, losing one's own body in the process by becoming invisible in the eyes of one's partner: this was totally outside the experience of everyday life as our centenarian knew it.

In 1966, Michel Foucault noted:

> Language was to surge up more and more insistently in a unity that we should have been able to but could not yet imagine. . . . Things and words would part company, the eye was henceforth destined to see and only to see, the ear to hear and only to hear. . . . From now on, language would accumulate without a point of departure, without an end and without promise. It is the traversal of this futile yet fundamental space that the literary text traces from day to day.

When the philosopher's *The Order of Things: An Archaeology of the Social Sciences* came out, work on automatic language processing had really been going on for a good thirty years already—since the concepts of cryptography and statistics had been put together after a lot of desultory tinkering, thus emphasizing the difference between natural language and artificial language, between tangible ideas and that which is merely "named."

When Foucault ponders *the crisis in size* at work in the architecture of language, one wonders what indeed, apart from some epistemological aberration, this afocal eye that would only see could be or this equally ignorant ear—unless we think of the prostheses and bodiless organs of our tools of transmission and investigation: radio, the telephone, the video surveillance camera, and now the exploded language of the computer. Everything *industrial mediatization* since the nineteenth century was supposed to be based on and that was supposed to make literature and the social sciences, scientific thought itself, subservient to the interpersonal schema of a minimal linguistic exchange, which would for a long time run on the dubious concept of "cause and effect" . . . as long as the question were worded correctly.

A TERMINAL ART

WITHOUT AN ESSENTIAL CULTURE OF disinformation, we might at least follow the advice of the ancient Stoic who recommended that a friend *not bring everything back to his eyes,* warning him against *sight's overflowing.* "The innumerable forms and images of visible things, let in one after the other, gather together and pile up at the bottom of the soul. . . . They weigh it down and worry it; the soul isn't made for this; it can't hold so many deformed objects. From this springs that *plague of phantoms* who dissipate our thoughts and whose pernicious variety bars the way to luminous contemplation."[1] *The ghosts won't starve, but we will perish.*

The confusing situation we find ourselves in with our communication technology is not unrelated to what we know from the study of road and industrial accidents. This is so even though we know that the military-industrial sphere and the business world, more indissociable than ever, here also do a perverse balancing act between the damage inflicted and subsequent reparation. In the nineteenth century, for instance, mass psychology develops with progress in military-industrial proletization and the necessary recourse to experimental methodology, statistics, and mathematical models. But in 1892, the factory inspectorate also appears, designed to oversee the protection of workers and especially women, children, and female minors. Around 1900, the consumer society starts to emerge in Europe along with an industrial cinema that General Ludendorff, mastermind of German strategy in 1917, considered "a veritable weapon"—well before Hitler or Mussolini. After 1918, work on the mental and physical traumas of victims of the first industrialized world war is undertaken, as well as more rigorous studies of accidents in the workplace and traffic accidents resulting from the *transport revolution.* The age of nuclear dissuasion finally completes the transmission revolution with the boom in commercial television.

Health workers in the United States and Canada, notably epidemiologists and pediatricians, would then identify a *televisual pathology* particularly affecting children and underprivileged communities said to be "at risk": abuse of television, following the depredations of slave labor, producing various morbid phenomena such as obesity or anorexia nervosa, poor cerebral performance, language problems, spatial disorientation, aggressiveness, alcoholism, and drug abuse. This work has dovetailed with the etiological research carried out by various U.S. federal organizations, casually putting murder up there as an epidemic, especially in the school environment, with 25,000 murders recorded in the United States in 1991.

In May 1992, a Harris poll conducted in France and published in *Santé Magazine,* also revealed a disturbing state of dependence in the mediatized: 43 percent of those interviewed claimed they would suffer if deprived of television, although 64 percent say they experience nausea after watching it. After twenty years of research into the pathology of television viewing in the United States, Victor S. Strasburger and S. Brandon Canterwell remark, "Even though it is difficult to contest the impact of television, we don't know how it works; no doubt we need to look to *qualitative methods* in order to understand it."[2]

Once more, *the lack of any means of defense when faced with the technological* is translated into cant, as Karl Kraus pointed out at the beginning of the century. Doesn't *"impact"* imply a certain energy, even if not that of mass? Why hide what is obvious—in a car accident, for instance—behind cultural rationalizations decisive elsewhere? Most of the time, though, even this type of traumatic shock also stems from informational pathology, from a certain deterioration in reception of audiovisual signals due to fatigue or abuse of alcohol or tranquilizers, which does not preclude taking into account the speed of the vehicle, speeding being penalized as a misdemeanor, that is, as a crime.

Who would now dream of giving a mass-produced automobile the form of a phaeton or some kind of horse-drawn cart, as they did around a hundred years ago? Who would now dream of giving a rocket a profile that was not aerodynamic and so would compromise its powers of penetration? Yet this is precisely what happens when one tries to impose an absolute dichotomy between the secondary effects of our *audiovisual vehicles* (their aesthetic, their ethics, their quality) and the electromagnetic wave trains that propel them at the speed of light. Just because the latter have no "corporeity," so to speak!

But to get back to our television pathology specialists. The case of the American *Stealth plane,* the F117—the prototype that has recently suffered a number of serious accidents after services rendered in the spectral Gulf War—should, surely, tell them something about the qualitative evolution and plasticity of our future audiovisual environment: *since what is seen is already destroyed, it's better to be destroyed before being seen* in the new optoelectronic war. This is why the F117 designers decided to abandon the old laws of physics governing aerodynamics and to opt instead for powers of penetration capable both of defying radar equipment's pencils of radio waves and of blinding the control screens. The phantom-plane is thus no longer content to emit lures in order to alter the enemy's field of perception. It is itself a *synthetic object* that anticipates the disappearance of its own image, the destruction of its representation.

Viewed in a direct observation field, at the Le Bourget Air Show in 1991, for example, the fearsome bomb-carrier, its chaotic silhouette smeared with some opaque substance, scarcely seems capable of taking off. But, while we are still at electronic iconography and the welter of digital imagery in "civilian" mode, Stealth is paving the way for an ultimate iconoclasm entirely cleansed of the contingencies of communication; it participates in a TERMINAL ART whereby the object itself restores the opacity of distancing, the blindness speed creates, of which the liberation of the media was supposed to have rid our vision of the world. The Americans are so convinced of this that they did not show their new prototypes, Stealth's successors, at the Le Bourget Air Show in 1993. But are we still talking aeronautics here?

We are reaching the end of a cycle of apperception. As I have written elsewhere, "Blindness is thus very much at the heart of the coming 'vision machine.' The production of sightless vision is itself merely the reproduction of an intense blindness that will become the latest and last form of industrialization: the industrialization of the non-gaze."[3] But let us not forget that before the invention of this ultimate "synthetic vision" that will allegedly deliver us from "the act of seeing," inventions like photographic instantaneity, Jules Janssen's astronomic revolver of 1832, the later chronophotographic gun of physiologist Jules-Etienne Marey that enabled the movement of objects traveling through space at great speed to be visualized, or, finally, the cinema motor of the scientific camera—all of these new apperceptual techniques essentially tended *to cover what was invisible to the naked eye with the mask of the visible.*

Through these innovations, our visual deficiency, our relative blindness, were transposed to representation's center stage, communication. This is why, of all the traditional visual arts, *illusionism* necessarily found itself at the origin of the retinal hallucination of the cinema motor—but also, equally, of its fantasmatic amplification through use of trick effects, cinema's latest special effects, and, finally, digital imagery.

Besides, the filiation is obvious, extending from Daguerre to the clock maker Robert Houdin, who used Daguerre's diorama idea to create shows in which the illusion was based directly on retinal persistence and who discovered what he called *"the specific tenses of vision,"* and to Georges Méliès, who invented special effects in film and was also the last director of Houdini's *Théâtre des soirées fantastiques* from 1888 to 1924. The art of illusionism is entirely based on putting the viewer's visual limitations to use by attacking his innate capacity to distinguish between the real and what he thinks is real and true, thereby getting him to believe in something that has never existed, *to believe in nothingness.*

Unlike Plato's magician, recreating the World at whim, the nineteenth-century illusionist can already invent not only bi- or trimorphic synthetic objects that prevent the spectator from being able to see everything. He can also set up a synthetic environment that forces the observer this time *to not see a thing.* It is all done with doors and especially with mirrors, those famous mirrors which, we might note, have begun to come into their own again in the latest

generation of optoelectronic military research. Taking his
cue from Houdin, it was, moreover, a military man, one
Colonel Stodare, who succeeded in making himself partly
invisible on stage in 1865. H. G. Wells was to publish his
novel *The Invisible Man* thirty years later; the director,
James Whale, aided by John Fulton on special effects,
brought off the film version, a cinematic masterpiece, in
1933, just before Méliès died. "This sort of stylish mystery,
a journey through the impossible," writes Paul Gilson,
"with raindrops alone betraying the man's silhouette and
turning him into a ghost in the colors of a prism, or a phantom trapped by a rainbow. The mist continues to circle
around his contours and the snow inexplicably bears the
trace of his footsteps . . . until the policeman fires at his
heart, until the invisible man *becomes splendidly visible
again in order to die.*"

Whereas the magicians of antiquity packed the stage
with a host of heteroclite objects, Houdin launched the
modern era of illusionism in asserting that "the fundamental principle of prestidigitation is to produce big effects using small means" . . . like a mechanic. He thus introduced a
sort of insidious antiphenomenology into techniques of
representation, a certain defeat of perceptual faith. The
great John Maskelyne would further refine Stodare's act.
Maskelyne himself was born into an old family that num-
bered astronomers, physicists, and other "mathemagi-
cians." Like Houdin, he made up androids, a "whist
player," a "typewriter." It was one of his descendants, Jasper Maskelyne, who transferred the art of illusion to the

battlefield, thereby contributing to Allied victory at El Ala-
mein in 1942, this time by creating, in the desert itself, a
synthetic ecology designed to baffle the enemy's means of
perception and promote the "false movements" of the British Army.

Even now, many of Jasper Maskelyne's inventions remain *classified,* that is, reserved for a restricted number of
initiates. Among other devices, he invented a system of in-
frared communication and a method of making planes invisible to anti-aircraft defense projectors at low altitude.
He also improved camouflage of artillery positions by using reflective surfaces and even—very close to Stealth—ad-
vocated application of an *omega gray* based on the color of
the petrel for camouflaging objects at sea. . . . [4]

For Maskelyne, dissimulation was unquestionably *central
to representation,* as the more powerful techniques of perception became, *the more the cancellation of reality would
spread,* from people to large-scale objects and finally to
whole regions.

Let's drop all the poppycock Westerners go in for when
it comes to art or representation and consider for a moment a phrase of Paul of Tarsus's: "The world we see is in
the process of passing." We might now add: "We cannot
see the world as it goes by." We cannot naturally perceive
its going slowly any more than we can perceive its speeding up, any more than we can perceive what might be the
reality of time itself in which movement occurs. *Movement
is blindness.*

So when the camera/motor ceases to produce an imitation of *real* movement at twenty-four images per second and begins to experiment with *abnormal speeds*—what Ray Harryhausen calls "dynamation" in contrast to the "animation" of the cartoon—the viewer shows signs of a certain disarray. He finds himself suddenly pushed to the limits of his capacity for visual identification by this recreation of the "mystery of movement," which is the primitive dimension of our perception of the world.

On a similar note, filmmaker Michael Powel says, "For me dance is and always has been part of cinema. . . . In *The Red Shoes,* I altered the speed in the same scene all the time. Twenty-four images a second is monotonous, so I went from forty-eight to six images a second, *which meant I could do all the special effects directly, on the set.*"

Bergson used to say, "There is more in immobility." Whence the notion that representation will essentially depend on, in the West, until the innovation of the motor: *immobility makes visible.* The plastic arts will come to immobilize movement, thereby *offering the illusion of seeing, of having the time to see.*

The cozy landscape of the *still life* was undoubtedly the most accomplished form of art, perhaps because its immobile world makes us dream of the repose in which the deceased becomes an exposed object that one can contemplate at leisure, taking one's time, since they are now still. We also have the very strong impression that the person who has stopped being alive exists more fully than when actually alive, moving around before us, producing an

overabundance of images of themselves. As in James
Whale's film: invisible while alive, the invisible man becomes magnificently visible again in dying.

In Vermeer, that most accomplished of painters, the living world is like a still life, an installation before the spectator's very eyes of a series of objects opposed to movement. If the painter were to disturb any one of these,
however slightly, in the course of his work, he knows that
not only this object, but all the rest will have changed identity by losing their placidity. Illustrating the words of the
Stoic, Schopenhauer writes on the subject of the Dutch
painter, "The viewer cannot look at Vermeer's paintings
without being moved, without imagining the mental state
of the artist, peaceful, calm, completely serene, exactly as
required by the job of focusing on ordinary, insignificant
objects and reproducing them so lovingly. This impression
is all the more marked when we return to ourselves and are
struck by the contrast between such calm and our own
eternally unfathomable feelings, forever churned up by desires and anxieties."[5]

From the beginning of the motor revolution, the starting
up of images ruined this stationary organization and, with
it, vision's repose, the pause of luminous contemplation,
"the field of presence in the wider sense" generating the visual disinformation that would soon reduce the processes
of representation and communication to their simplest
forms.

We now know that we can exhaust the world's being, so
why not anticipate that we can also rapidly exhaust the

fragile sphere of our dreams, our fantasies, our amazements—which no one is now presenting as the ultimate goal of a civilization that would actually end up experimenting with them?

But the works of the Surrealists, particularly their famous "Dream Bank," showed us the poverty of the trivial dream, which is so curiously lacking in variety and imagination that the representation of our desires becomes a load of drivel, with endless repetition of a few limited themes. The same thing can be said of digital imagery, which merely imitates the special effects and tricks of the old 3D cinema or animated cartoon, while ostensibly running up against the plastic limits of the imagination.

What we are seeing here is indeed the consequence and conclusion of the old quarrel between documentary filmmakers and pictorialists at the turn of the century: should the synthetic image imitate film or can it have its own mode of existence proper, in the manner in which scientific photography takes its distance from pictorial representation? We have clearly reached the point of no return here, with a major question about what now appears to be an abuse of language. Although determined to prove the opposite, creative man is not for all that a *creator; creation* is not his realm, and though so often used, the word creator is inappropriate. In a sense, man is more definitely an engineer. Following on from the Futurists, Duchamp and the kineticists and other partisans of general motorization proved the point: twentieth-century art has no more future than twenty-first-century technoscience will have. The ruining of its stationary organization merely revealed *that tendency to chaos,* which, according to Schlegel, *is hidden in all ordered creation.*

Recent Canadian and American research offers an idea of the pathology and all-too-real effects produced by running images at high or variable speeds past people with a tendency to dyslexia: in general these subjects do not see more than one in two images that would normally be picked up by natural vision's stereoscopic organization. Dimensions, depth, volume, and spatiality are poorly perceived compared to color and outline. The latter disappear at very high projection speeds—the viewer can no longer see anything. The theory that dyslexia is just a defect of the language center, that is, of the social relief of communication, is accordingly ditched. Dyslexia also affects the intelligible construction of appearances, our innate ability to make a distinction between the real and the images we construct of it.

Recently a well-known couturier declared, "Today, luxury has come to mean the right to mix, to pile it on, *to refuse to choose.*" The gaze no longer chooses where to rest, because from now on we can look anywhere, everywhere, or nowhere, since in constructing images proper to sight, volumes, values, and distances are cruelly lacking. We might further note that said couturier's designs, with their jarring asymmetry and strident colors, are a faithful enough reproduction of the ultimate identification phase of a dyslexic version of reality.

* * *

Since instantaneity was invented and the cinema motor put into spin, our era has progressed in leaps and bounds toward the end of a cycle of appearance—meaning not only directly observable appearances, but, lately, those of indirect perception. And we have not batted an eye over the succession of demolition jobs: the demise of the old image motor as undisputed witness of the world's movement and the overtaking of our visual limitations by the blinding penetrative power of electromagnetic waves. These only "bring into the world" the very essence of media violence—the terrorist aesthetic of optical impact that now emerges increasingly insistently on our monitor screens as on the screens of popular television, with the avowed aim of transforming the observer or viewer into an agent or potential victim, as in war.

Brad Nunk, an American specializing in synthetic images at Angel Studio, recently said, "Like sex and blood, special effects have become an indispensable ingredient in making a blockbuster."

Apropos of communications technology, the old law is thus being borne out: the faster the announcement effect, the more the announcement becomes *accidental* and *insubstantial*.

Like the erstwhile theater show, radio, cinema, and television aimed to arouse *natural* emotions such as anger, surprise, distress, anticipation (desire). But only pending the *artificial* effects of the paroxysmal acceleration of representational techniques. Tetanization, vertigo, overexcitement, a state of shock will evacuate all judgment, any system of rational evaluation, any positive, negative, or even simply deleterious selection of messages and images. Having become contingent, the announcement effect will soon be reduced to a simple frequency signal, an impulse that can dispense with any concern for plausibility. Proper training of the younger generation is already ensured through the success of video games exclusively based on the virtuality of disappearance and elimination—reflex games that can induce a total loss of consciousness in photosensitive subjects similar to the orgasmic effects of epilepsy.

Since *technological generations* succeed each other, the man of the *written word* (books, the press) can no more recognize his son of the *screen* generation (cinema, television) than the latter can recognize his own vid-kid, prey to the tyranny of video.[6]

The incredible events that have recently overturned the world geopolitical situation have shed further light on this problematic. In the East, for instance, was it the freedom or the liberation of the press that was involved at the end of the 1980s? *Freedom?* Surely not, or if so, then under tight surveillance, since unnamed sponsors and film directors kept themselves planted firmly behind microphones and cameras. *Liberation?* Surely, for it was not so much events that got out of hand, as claimed, but, indeed, the technology of fact transmission, the intensivity of this twenty-four hours a day prohibiting any objective control, any genuine expertise, and abruptly disqualifying the representatives of an information complex now technically obsolete.

All this foreshadowing the Gulf War, which no one would compare to a video game, a *war game*. And the extensive blackout ordered by the Pentagon, imposing silence on photographers, reporters, journalists, and the usual commentators of the print and electronic media. The American military machine had decided that the new arsenal of *communication weapons* should "speak" in their place as *ultima ratio,* as information's final, explosive argument.

A long time after the likes of Lakanal, Carnot, and Bonaparte, there can be no doubt that the media were, once again, being taken in hand by a military-information complex continually at the cutting edge of technological progress. Lagging behind the war and soon to be cobbled by the economic recession, the "fourth estate" was on the way to becoming itself MEDIATIZED. In 1994, a new television station, the *Military Channel,* will actually come into being in the United States; this will broadcast documentaries on arms and war, as well as series and features with a military theme, twenty-four hours a day.

VICTIMS OF THE SET

I saw, taking shape under the midday sun,
a cheerless society that lies.

PAUL MORAND

DURING THE FIRST WORLD WAR, the great art
dealer René Gimpel took advantage of France's wartime
prestige to bring European art to a good number of filthy
rich American industrialists who wanted to build collec-
tions or foundations.

In the course of his first tour of America, Gimpel thus
had occasion to discover a migrant population whose principal cultural reference was an art for art's sake of technical
effectiveness virtually unknown in Europe, "a materialism
that took the form of a cult of the machine that was,
strictly speaking alarming, in makeshift villages no longer
centered on a church or a temple, but on a factory, a mine-
shaft, or a railway station, and often deserted overnight."[1]

Without such precedents, Hollywood, the world capital
of the cinema motor, might never have existed as Cendrars

describes it in 1936 in a series of articles for the newspaper *Paris-Soir*: a forbidden city in the state of California, a state under siege, patroled by three police divisions responsible for mercilessly ousting undesirables: sick people or germ-carriers hoping to benefit from the temperate climate, and especially the unemployed, the single women, and the abandoned children who had come to stamp their feet and sink at the doors of vast studio factories, sealed off like fortresses, before finally being sent back to their state of origin or imprisoned in concentration camps in the middle of the desert.[2]

"Except perhaps for Monte Carlo, there isn't a town in the world where people commit suicide as much as they do in Hollywood," Cendrars notes, "this Hollywood that's like Cannes, Luna Park, and Montparnasse all rolled into one, a marvelous improvisation, a spontaneous, continuous, endless spectacle, put on in the street night and day in front of the set of America that serves as backdrop." The writer-journalist was certainly not taken in. During his interminable crossing of the American continent from east to west, he had a sudden illumination; this particular train trip reminded him of another: "Where was I? No, it wasn't possible! I really was in a train, in America, in the twentieth century! And not in the middle of the eighteenth century, in a telega, crossing the steppes of the Ukraine on Catherine the Great's unforgettable trip to Crimea."

What Cendrars made out through the window of his compartment suddenly looked to him something like "the famous mobile sets Prince Potemkin had ranged along the horizon, the entire length of his sovereign's itinerary, to give her a false impression of how civilized and prosperous her immense empire was!

"What a great joke! *But who was supposed to be hood-winked here in this democracy, if not the sovereign people?"*

A mobile people entirely *victims of the set,* a democracy that had had its head turned by the optical illusion of the *ever-changing skyline.* The dynamics of the landscape glimpsed are a mere sham, a very deliberate and elaborate sham. All media basically form one single medium, from the telega in the Ukrainian steppes to the transcontinental rail and the cinema motor city, where cars already out-number people and where anyone strolling about on foot is suspect.

"*Don't stay here!* Fly, spread out over the whole country, go west, young man!" Last century's oracles are silent, the trompe l'oeil journey ends at the Pacific; Hollywood with its studio factories is the terminus, the last stop where the next stage of the trip is already on the drawing board: the *industrialization of perception,* the ultimate coup d'état.

In Europe, while the first socialists were dreaming of bringing down the class structure, railway companies were inaugurating a new class structure, *the speed classes.* The well-heeled traveler could take a "first-class" train that of-fered him not only the luxury of comfort, but more than this, the totally unprecedented luxury of *going fast.* He could do the Paris-Fécamp trip, for example, in three

hours and forty-eight minutes (Fécamp then being a luxury seaside resort). It would take the second-class train
traveler four hours and forty-four minutes; the third-class
passenger, six or seven hours or more. Around 1900, the
third-class Paris-Marseille train took twenty-eight hours
or more to reach the Phoenician city, whereas the first-
class *rapide* could do the same trip in sixteen hours. The
rapidity of train travel would then be seen as an effective
treatment for those disoriented souls infected by hatred of
the near and present world—the *Weltschmerz* of waning
romanticism—for whom, as the German term *Langweile*
suggests, time seemed to practically stand still, passing
desperately slowly and producing a slowing down of psy-
chomotor function that prevented them from moving
about of their own accord.

A habitué of train travel, Flaubert writes, "I loathe
movement." But elsewhere he notes, "I want to see
Lapland, India, Australia. The world is so beautiful! Fancy
dying and not seeing half of it!" This is not a contradiction;
for Flaubert, life is only bearable *as long as you are never in
it,* which is what happens in the serious epileptic fits that
convince him he has "died several times." But also that he
has come back from the other side. In *The Temptation of
Saint Anthony,* he writes further, "Aren't you tired of this
body that weighs on your soul and cramps it like a narrow
cell would? Demolish the flesh, then . . . we shun the flesh,
we execrate it." To expand, to dissolve, become weightless,
burst, leave one's heavy body behind: our whole destiny
could now be read in terms of escape, of evasion. To be *un-*

happy in one's skin, as in a shagreen, or in a coat that's too tight and pulls at the sleeves (mass, congestion, span), a coat too heavy for the person doomed to wear it, to move it. As though there were a radical incompatibility between the size of the envelope of flesh the subject is decked out in and the space-time, without knowable beginning or end, of his being in the world—birth and death, objects of belief, eluding immediate consciousness; or between *internal horizons* easily conceived as gaping (*unding* = deprived of meaning) and the real horizon of the world which, Merleau-Ponty tells us, *we approach initially through sight.*

The great joke of steam train acceleration already implied numerous means of "demolishing the flesh"; by boring right through the external horizon, transport's optical illusion had the power to transform it into chasms, then abysses, soon as gaping as those of our internal horizons. One could then speak of acceleration as the *temptation of the heavy being,* with the perceived world's conversion into a series of abysses, *the end of the world* in which, after Flaubert's saint, every individual could cry out before the progressive expansion of the nothingness of the universe: "A gulf behind me, a gulf before me, to the right, to the left, above, below, darkness everywhere!"

Rapidity is always a sign of precocious death for the fast species. The mechanical overload that accompanies strenuous muscular exertion is for man, as for other vertebrates that show celerity in hunting or eluding predators, the source of many physical traumatisms. It is also an important factor in aging. At the onset of the industrial age, workers died young, worn out by the frenzied pace of daily slave labor and by the physical effort involved in getting around. The armies of the mass wars of the end of the eighteenth century and of the beginning of the nineteenth lost more men during endless forced marches than on the battlefield. Conversely, with the mechanization of production and transport, the average human life span would increase, thanks partly to a certain slowing down of the individual's motor impulse, to reduced physical effort.

By placing a longer lifespan within reach of the majority, the motor created a new perception of time—the perception of *too much time, time to spare*, linked to the heavy body's reduced amount of movement and to the different nature of its motor activities, a certain disorientation which, by relativizing our actions, also relativized our thinking.

As their civilization evolved, the ancient Greeks shifted the seat of the soul from its primitive location in the heart, that organ so called upon during physical exertion, and raised it to the brain. This was no doubt a matter of bringing a new solution to bear on the *oscillation in size* to which man's body has been involuntarily subject since the dawn of time. From this point on, the "conscious" being claimed to exert authority over his dimensional costume, much as he enjoyed exerting authority over the surrounding territory in an industrious society that also happened to practice slavery and in which the life expectancy of the elite shot up along with their expectations.

Those expectations, stemming from reduction or relativization of movement, were then thought to be an attentional phenomenon. It is amusing to think that philosophy would have appeared locally, almost naturally, not as just "a major inquiry about time" (Bachelard), but, more pragmatically, as an inquiry about the new freedom *to give substance to lengthening time.*[3]

The familiar story goes that the ancient sage enjoyed a long life, dying the way slow species die, at an advanced age, over a hundred years old—unless he chose to slough off this mortal coil voluntarily.

Maybe philosophy is just idle (often pointless) curiosity, born of the disappearance of physical effort once this becomes unnecessary.

The reasoning of the healthy mind *(logos)* is not merely the art of accepting the inevitable; beyond this, for the Stoic, it is *an eternal property,* a remedy against the scantiness of our dimensional lot. The seeker of wisdom, says Seneca, is not afraid of annexing all past and future ages to his own; through his works, he has access to the whole range, none are out of bounds: "By lifting up our souls, we can enjoy a vast period of time through which to stretch ourselves."[4]

On the other hand, when the great Roman City was enslaved by its slaves and mercenaries, the Stoic would warn of the dangers weighing on thought and the mind's tranquillity, of a confusion in motor function that was nothing more than a form of overindulgence, of incontinence on the part of whoever approaches the world through sight

only, bringing everything back to his eyes, victim of the excessive gratuitousness of human movement. "There are
certain things that delight our body even while causing it a
sort of pain, such as turning over in bed and changing sides
well before that side is tired and constantly changing positions to cool off. . . . Hence, men go on pointless trips and
wander about faraway shores; fickle, never satisfied with
the present, they try land one minute, the sea the next.
They go on one trip after another and from one spectacle to
the next. . . . This," says Seneca, "is where disgust with life
and the world itself starts, and in the mad delirium of their
own self-indulgence, the pleasure seeker cries out: *when
will it ever be just the same old thing?*"[5]

This recalls the little-known story in the Bible where Jacob stays up "until the breaking of the day" *measuring
himself* against *some incommensurable being,* without either one letting go. The particular *someone* whom Jacob
cannot manage to shake off is perhaps neither an angel, nor
God, but Jacob himself, overcome with contempt for his
own size and, after a night of furious struggle, forced to acknowledge the limits of his own body, "that unbearable fel-
low traveler who won't be left behind."

Already the world searched in vain is merely a narrow
couch, the most far-ranging travels a series of tiny movements that, instead of wearying, delight the drowsy body.
Unless, that is, the power of inertia in the end manages to
transform the pleasure seeker into the living dead, driving
him into forgetting who he is, to the point where he needs
someone else to tell him where he is, and in what position,

like the Roman who asked his slaves, as he clambered out of the bath and flopped onto his sedan, "Am I sitting down yet?"

The current progress in transport and transmission has only exacerbated this unremarked pathology of movement that takes place no longer between here and there, but between *being there* and *no longer being there*. From the elimination of the physical effort of walking to the sensorimotor loss induced by the first fast transport, we have finally achieved states bordering on sensory deprivation. We have come a long way from the first open railway carriages—borrowed for the fairground, jolting you about on hard wooden seats, the cold and the wind whipping around you, blinding clouds of smoke covering you with soot—to the TGV and the supersonic cell, where you are shut off from the outside world that you make such a dreadful racket, though, zooming across.

The loss of the thrills of the old voyage is now compensated for by the showing of a film on a central screen. The voyager continues to approach the world through sight, but this time it is the cinema motor that reinvents for us the passing parade of a landscape that disappears and freezes in the distancing brought on by altitude.

In the middle of the transport revolution of the nineteenth century, Jules Michelet predicted, "Every climate is a remedy; the medicine of the future will be a judicious emigration movement." Michelet accordingly recommends that society dames flee their habitual abode and "imitate birds migrating ahead of the sun." He warns his "dear boredom-sufferers," though, against the speed of the express train: "It is most unwise for an excitable person to go from Paris to the Mediterranean in twenty hours, passing through completely different climates from one hour to the next." Last century's health-based emigration already posited a *new calendar,* one required this time by a geotropical race determined by the Earth's spinning on its axis.

A master of Pereire and Lesseps, Count Saint-Simon notes, "The planet depends on the Universe. It is like a pendulum inside a clock whose movement is communicated to it. Man depends on the planet he inhabits; he is like a watch inside a pendulum inside a clock." It will not be long before the acceleration in transport and transmission allowed by Saint-Simon's own disciples unhinges clock, pendulum, and watch alike. Michelet's invalids dodge the seasons of an out-of-date calendar and do so every morning at that; in the Transiberian, Cendrars puts his watch back *since the train is going forward while the sun is hanging back.* Producing an unprecedented amount of movement, the innovation of the motor *provided in one stroke what time only grants a bit at a time* (Morand). It will see to it that Earth's inhabitants get used to visiting the planet not as beings subject to physical laws, prisoners of Saint-Simon's clock anymore, but as rebels, marginals, escapees.

The nineteenth century provided few technical means for escaping the material conditions of an existence that was still played out fairly slowly or for maintaining the luxury of travel time that would use up the time of one's earthly sojourn.

Nicknamed "The Locomotive Empress," Elizabeth of the Austro-Hungarian Empire took off for nearly three hundred days a year, traipsing from Corfu to Venice, from the Carpathians to the Riviera. Yet being perpetually whisked away by train was not enough to cure her of physiological disgust for her own heavy body. She thus decided once and for all that, being five-feet-eight inches tall, she would weigh no more than a hundred and ten pounds forever after and so restricted herself to a diet of milk and oranges, in other words, to an absolute fast, thereby launching a fashion that would later take off in a big way.

In 1843, Heinrich Heine notes, "The railway obliterates space, all we have left is time. If only we had enough money to kill the latter in a convenient manner!" The money would be found, and lots of it. It would first be spent at tourist spots, seaside resorts, and in the *delocalization of the local* that consists of frittering away the appearances of the real world in a series of temporary sets. Alongside Nature's being *taken in hand* by scientific and industrial materialism would be its *mise-en-scène* by a cosmopolitan elite. Of the two utopias, the second would prove the most tenacious; it would be the one to ultimately bring about present-day society as we know it—the ultimate form of colonial exhaustion, endocolonization that has survived decolonization itself.

Beaches or mountaintops: the preferred playgrounds of
this final civilization rather resemble the nihilist camp of
Julien Gracq's warriors, those prowlers of city fringes,
lounge lizards of the apocalypse, living free from material
cares on the edge of their domesticated ravines—and off
the locals, whom they offend with their loose morals and
beliefs. International tourism currently recreates this colonial violence, with the introduction of holiday clubs and
luxury hotels that now look like advanced posts in places
mostly poverty stricken and hostile.

But we must not forget that without fast ships there
would be no trading posts, without trains no significant
tourist resorts, without cars and planes, no worldwide commercial tourism. At first glance, though, it may seem para-
doxical that *Langweile,* the repeated sensation that time is
standing still, could find relief in a motor, a machine, which
by definition only produces the same, invariably repeating
itself. Unless the dilemma is resolved by precisely the one
variation the motor is capable of: *acceleration.* The question of engine speed, however, carries its own limits and
therefore a specific *Langweile* due to the *final exhaustion of
time* by speed, just as Heine suggested.

It seems this might explain why the choice destinations
of this last civilization, from the nineteenth century on,
have been places *at the end of the line*—in the case of tourist resorts, mountaintops and coastal spots in an unstable
telluric state, subject to perpetual metamorphosis. Some
time in the 1920s, a young servant girl, seeing the ocean for
the first time one day in a storm, waxes lyrical about the

power of the mounting tide: "Madame," she says to her mistress, "there must be such an enormous engine inside to move all that!"

Stripped of a romanticism not of its own making, the sea appeared to the girl to be a gigantic machine at work. In which she was not wrong, since sea (and mountain) demonstrate the major themes of classical mechanics—kinetics and dynamics—in their natural state: the ocean, able to cast bodies into a state of seeming weightlessness and to carry and quickly shift heavy engines; mountains, in their sheerness and obliquity, able to cause the high speed of the free fall, of slipping. We used to go to the very motivity of the geological landscape to recover not so much health as some hypothetical deliverance from our own bodies. The actor Klaus Kinski once said, "At sea, you can hardly tell the difference between being born and dying."

A new materialism was clearly at work here, one arising from a dromological (or dromoscopic) conception of the World: from the *Enlightenment,* the fires of artillery and the steam engine had blazed into history transforming physics and soon "natural philosophy." The physicist Sadi Carnot, son of the great Lazare Carnot, published his reflections on the motor power of fire in 1824, thus heralding thermodynamics, the theory that was to overturn the entire set of sciences of matter, space, and time and wind up in the twentieth century in *a dynamic global vision* of the Earth and its biosphere, in a global ecosystem.

They say the American pioneer spirit consisted in "consuming available space with a voracity unique in the history of human migratory movements." However, the cosmopolitan elite anticipated this swallowing up that each and every one of us is living today, with its pivotal undermining of any sense of the usefulness of humanity now that we have lost any productive relationship with the environment, with a planet that will soon be no more than a way station, an abandoned construction site. In the century of the proletariat, tourist resorts celebrated motor incoherence ahead of the event and with it, the fatal gratuitousness of our acts.

Beach games have a symbolic significance, most often an introverted one. Regattas, polo, golf, tennis, a whole host of sports that were originally colonial or indigenous would develop exponentially precisely because they serve no purpose—except to kill lengthening time. We might note once more the polyvalency of the word *resort* [in French, *station*]. These are not villages in the process of development or new cities where people have come to settle down, but provisional stops along the way in a general displacement. One might begin by stopping for a year or two, then for a season (peak or off-peak), and, finally, with the acceleration in transport, for a month, a few days, a weekend, a few hours to "test the waters" . . .

At the end of his life, Flaubert notes indignantly that Parisians have brought with them to Trouville "chalets in the style of d'Enghien, artificial rocks for their gardens." This way of preserving the suburban milieu as a palliative to being uprooted was evident in the colonies and also, equally, in the United States. It would not last long. Soon, *to build* would also mean *to leave,* in the manner of the *diorama* whose cinematic realism subjected the nineteenth-century voyager to such a rough ordeal. (Chateaubriand writes, "How was I to know they were going to bring Jerusalem and Athens to Paris?") Or, later, the Moorish casinos of Arcachon, the Babylonian luxury hotels of the Côte d'Azur or the tropical gardens of the Isle of Batz. Many works have been devoted to such places of leisure (*licere* = to be permitted), where the norms of the *permissive society* began to take shape only to be popularized by the different mass media . . . *a cheerless society that lies, under the midday sun,* as Morand describes it at the end of his life. The bourgeois family falls apart at the seams; changing partners becomes acceptable, adultery is more readily tolerated; bodies expose themselves, shedding the weight of clothes and soon liberated from corsets; physical differences between the sexes diminish; one runs around "grooving" twenty-four hours a day, feverish, excited, tugged in all directions, hyperactive. In the 1980s, a Catalonian member of the Club of Rome named Perer Duran Farell was moved to say in an interview, "Man has stopped being an inhabitant of the planet. He has become a child of the universe. . . . All man's rational capacities can be transferred to a machine, so the rational side has become the least noble part of man. What's left? We still have our feelings, our freedoms, our contradictions, our anarchic impulses, our need for love, the necessity for what we think of as absurd."

What else could be left but absurdity and derision when one is completely caged by an idleness crammed with futile pursuits? More specifically, what is left of that healthy reason that was the art of making the best of a bad job and of mastering expectations of what might be, when *speeding* is precisely elimination of expectation and duration? Shifting the soul this time from the brain to the motor will free man from apprehension about a future that no longer has any raison d'être, since everything is already there, here and now, present and over at once, in the instantaneous apocalypse of messages and images, in the great old joke of the end of the world! After the disappearance of shifting horizons, what is left is the natural energy of *stops at the end of the line.* So as ultimate cure for *Langweile,* fringe civilization can propose "extremist sports," which are in fact sports of *the last extremity.* Dr. Touzeau claims:

> Through behavior equivalent to a suicide attempt, such as anorexia or drug addiction, but also high-risk conduct like speeding, riding a motorbike without a helmet, straight-line windsurfing, and so on, the individual thinks he can dominate the idea that he is weak. This confrontation with limits has its background in the classic fantasy of wanting to completely dominate one's destiny. The professional approach in this case is to send the subject back to words rather than acts.

A difficult return to communication and the logos in a depressive culture where technological acceleration means that departure and arrival—birth and death—blur to such an extent that they look the same. The term *breakdown* (interruption, descent) clearly illustrates the interaction of the dysfunctioning and sudden collapse involved in depression.

From now on *you do not climb, you fall.* In a once deserted part of Normandy, tens of thousands of tourists of all ages reinvoke every summer the curse of the *fall of the angels* by hurling themselves into the void from the top of the pylons of the viaduct over the Souleuvre in front of video cameras (as indispensable here as anywhere else), "bungee jumping," repeated simulations of the ultimate getting off, anticipating a *near death experience.*

Neurologist Didier Vincent recently remarked, "The brain doesn't like boredom, so it switches off—through sport, sex, leisure activities, drugs." To this modestly exhaustive list we might add the search for limit situations or the pleasure of seeing blood, whether of animals or people, a sure sign of the beginning of worldwide civil war and the banalization of private terrorism.

What these various ways of switching off indicate above all is the spectacular progress of a lifestyle in which everyone is now working on departure, in the footsteps of the old extravagant cosmopolitan elite. The liberating power of the media in the end has led to frequent and violent attempts to interrupt conscious life. We might compare what Didier Vincent has to say with the claims of Michel Imbert, of the Pierre and Marie Curie University, who argues the *plasticity of the brain,* pointing to a neuronal activity that can rebuild itself or destroy itself, according to the nature and range of the subject's sensory experiences, blocking or promoting reflection of the kind that leads to *delayed action* or anticipation, notably in the spheres of innovation and invention.

If we select competitive sport from among the various ways of switching off proposed by Vincent, we notice that the goal of training is synchronization of movement to the detriment of diachronization. It is now a matter of severely limiting *time for conscious intervention* on the part of the subject, to the point where the body seems to act of its own accord, without the aid of reflection, oblivious to the present world and so freed from doubt and hesitation.

Top sportspeople are not supposed to lose time listening to themselves think. They no longer take their own counsel; they listen instead to their video monitor while waiting for the automatic piloting of the car race and the times of the radio-controlled champion cyclist. Dr. Michael Prüfer, hero of a new discipline known as *kilomètre lancé (KL)*, or speed skiing, reached 229 kilometers an hour in the Winter Olympics of 1992. To attain this result, our new superman tested his clothes and attitudes in a wind tunnel under Renault's supervision, like a car. He appears on the track, head clapped in a helmet shaped like a cockpit, body squeezed into a translucent plastic cladding like a second skin, a speed-skin, which it takes him several hours to get into, as it is supposed to stick like glue. "My performances are 50 percent technical," he tells us. "Training in car tunnels is old hat now, anyway; we now need to look to aeronautic wind tunnels." He adds, "I don't play sport, I play speed. . . . *You don't think, you only think about going fast!*"

Henri de Montherlant played a lot of sports when he was young. He recalled, "I was a bit half-hearted at soccer, but in running I gave my all. . . . I specialized in the hundred meters—a race for idiots, which is why I was good at it!" Soccer does not require loss of consciousness the way the hundred-meter sprint does, with the runner having *to go like a rocket* in order to arrive almost instantaneously. Yet impresario Marcel Maréchal reckons, "Soccer is a beautiful sport, basic and quite moronic, for, unlike football, you play only with your feet—*and feet aren't as smart as hands!*"

Repetition of such practices ruins one's physical health in the long run, as is obvious with what happens to steroid-stuffed athletes. It can also lead to profound cerebral imbalance, a lack of judgment comparable to that of Seneca's zombie who can no longer remember much who he is or where he might happen to be.

As you will have gathered, *to disconnect is to disinform oneself.* If we believe what Michel Imbert claims regarding the brain's plasticity (its ability to rebuild itself or destroy itself according to the number and quality of the subject's sensory experiences), then the postindustrial world could not deconstruct itself all on its own and the spread of practices encouraged by the redoubtable *Weltschmerz* could very well soon turn an affair of neurons into an affair of state!

When, at the beginning of the century, Paul Morand boasts of belonging to "the great secret society of layabouts enjoying the scorn of a world which works too hard," it will not be for long. Just after the first paid holidays, Morand was to write a small manual, *For the Use of the New Idle;* he would soon worry, as Schopenhauer had before him, about the future of a world in which the forces of law and order and the state would need to watch out for civil wars fomented more by boredom than by poverty.

The industrial claim to the *"three eights"* (eight hours' work, eight hours' sleep, eight hours' leisure), so dear to the revolutionaries of 1848, cropped up just after the first railway links to the Channel coast were laid. Later, André François Ponchet noted regarding this eight-hour regimen: "It has all the advantages of a revolutionary revindication without the drawbacks or the peculiar merit of forging unity between all parties, from moderates to extremists."

Who indeed, among those in power, whether politicians or newspapermen, could find fault with the legitimization of the right to switch off sixteen hours a day, a right that was to end up fatally in the *quiet legalization of disinformation,* in total mediatization?

About forty years ago, the rabid commercialization of television, in democratizing access to the limit speed of electromagnetic waves, would bring about *the disappearance of the old speed classes.*

In modern democracies, the transmission revolution reenacted last century's revolution in industrial transport. The dysfunctional society of the ghetto soon reflected that of the waterside towns and obsolete enclaves that rail travel had created. Modern *tourists of desolation* have re-

placed the tourists of spleen, of tuberculosis or neurae-
sthenia who haunted the seaside resorts of the nineteenth
century, in the grip of hatred of the present world. Unemployment, anomie, and the most dire poverty have led to
an idleness comparable to that produced by wealth or disease, to flight as far away as possible from a familiar world
that really has become unhealthy and unlivable.

Tourists of desolation, like the Albanians who landed
half-naked and luggageless on the hostile coasts of Mezzo-
giorno, the most poverty-stricken region of the European
Community, only to realize they had been had and that the
land of milk and honey shown on Western TV never existed. Asked why he had emigrated, one such stray said he
had seen an ad for catfood on Italian TV. The fact of serv-
ing a small animal food on a silver platter goaded him irre-
sistably into leaving home. *If that's how they treat animals,
imagine how they treat human beings?*

The response to advertising's new take on geopolitics
was provided by former President Andreotti: "Italy cannot
possibly accommodate the thousands of Albanians besieg-
ing our coasts." The hordes of hopeful voyagers would be
mercilessly parked in Victoria Stadium before being sent
home. To calm them down and get them on buses detailed
to take them to the airport, all that was needed was to
make them think they would be flying to the United States.

According to a recent UNESCO report, in 1993, 120 million people in the world live outside the borders of their
country of origin.

FROM SUPERMAN TO
HYPERACTIVE MAN

What matters most to modern man is no longer pleasure or displeasure, but excitement.

NIETZSCHE

THE TECHNOLOGY QUESTION IS INSEPARABLE from the question of *where* technology occurs. Just as it is impossible to understand NATURE without immediately tackling the question of the LIFE-SIZE, we cannot now talk about technological progress without immediately considering size, the dimensions involved in the new technologies.

After yesterday's *superstructure* and *infrastructure,* we might now envisage a third term, *intrastructure,* since the very recent advent of nanotechnological miniaturization promotes biotechnology's physiological intrusion into, or insemination of, the living organism.

Having contributed for a long time already to the colonization of the geographical expanse of the *territorial body* and the geological core of our planet, the recent progress in

99

science and technoscience has today resulted in the gradual colonization of the organs and entrails of man's *animal body,* the invasion of the microphysical finishing off the job that the geophysical invasion began. This is the latest political figure in a process of domestication which, having genetically altered animal species and socially conditioned human populations, now heralds the age of personal components.

Today, indeed, the place *where state-of-the-art technology occurs* is no longer so much the limitless space of an infinitely vast planetary or cosmic environment, but rather the infinitesimal space of our internal organs, of the cells that compose our organs' living matter.

The loss or, more precisely, decline of the *real space* of every expanse (physical or geophysical) to the exclusive advantage of no-delay *real-time* teletechnology, inevitably leads to the *intraorganic intrusion of technology and its micromachines into the heart of the living.*

The end of the primacy of the relative speeds of mechanical transport and the sudden primacy of the absolute speed of electromagnetic transmission annihilates, along with the expanse and duration of our world proper, the ontological privilege of the body INDIVI, of this "body proper," which is in turn subject to the assault of technology, a molecular breaking and entering by biotechnologies capable of peopling its guts and very soul. At the end of the millennium, the miniaturization of motors, transmitter-receivers, and sundry other microprocessors is thus central to the technology question and thereby to postindustrial DESIGN.

After the industrial revolution and the revolution in instantaneous transmission of the age of large-scale mass communications, the very latest of revolutions is now taking off: the TRANSPLANT revolution, the power of inhabiting or, rather, of supplying the vital body through technologies of stimulation, as though physics (microphysics) were gearing up to compete with the chemistry of nutrition and mood-altering substances.

From time immemorial, technological progress generally has been directed to molding Earth's horizon and the continental surface, with the invention of hydraulic systems, canals, bridges, and roads—*megamachines* whose purpose was the railway lines and highways they carved the land up into, thanks to urban centers' being equipped with electric wiring and cables, electricity embellishing what the revolution in physical displacement had already achieved. Now the inner core of the living is to be equipped with micromachines that can effectively stimulate our faculties. The disabled person equipped to overcome his handicap suddenly becomes the model for the able-bodied person superequipped with prostheses of all descriptions. . . .

It is time we faced facts. If the invention of nutrition and varied eating habits led in the past to an "art of living" and of enduring, thanks to agricultural, then urban, sedentariness, the current redefinition of nutritional practices through ingestion not only of *chemical* but also of *technological* stimulants, will soon promote a behavioral mutation that will undoubtedly shape living conditions. The METADESIGN of postindustrial social practices and behavior will then take over where the industrial era's DESIGN of forms and objects left off. At the end of his life, in *Ecce Homo,* Nietzsche said, "I am much more interested in a question on which the 'salvation of humanity' depends far more than on any theologian's curio: the question of nutrition. For ordinary use, one may formulate it thus: '*How do you, among all people, have to eat to attain your maximum of strength, of virtue?*' "[1] The technosciences are beginning to provide their answer to that question. Following the ingestion of food to fortify our strength—the fruits of agriculture—they are gearing up to make us swallow, to feed us, all kinds of dope. Not just *chemical* substances after the modern fashion in stimulants such as alcohol, coffee, tobacco, drugs, and steroids, but also *technological* substances, the products of biotechnology, such as the *intelligent chips* that are allegedly able to superexcite our mental faculties. In 1838, Honoré de Balzac wrote, "Every form of excess is based on some pleasure that man wishes to repeat beyond the normal laws laid down by Nature. *The less human strength is occupied, the more it tends to excess.* It follows that the more civilized and peaceful a society is, the more its members will embark on the path to excess. *For man the social animal, living means expending one's energy pretty swiftly.*"[2]

One could not find a more accurate description of postmodernity's inventory, in which superstimulants are the logical extension of a metropolitan sedentariness that is spreading increasingly rapidly, thanks in particular to the teleaction that has once and for all supplanted immediate action. Postmodern man's inertia, his passivity, demands a surplus of excitement not only through patently unnatural sports practices, but also in habitual activities in which the body's emancipation due to real-time remote-control technology eliminates the traditional need for physical strength or muscular exertion.

Ultimately, the invention of the pacemaker, which can reproduce and in fact supply the rhythm of life, might be considered a starting point for this type of biotechnological innovation. Following the "xenotransplant" of animal organs, it is now on to the "technotransplant," that mix of the technological and the living, organic heterogeneity no longer involving attaching a *foreign body* to the patient's own. Now what is attached is a *foreign heartbeat* that can make the body throb in time to the machine.

Once this happens, how can we possibly assume that things will remain in working order? That this sudden overstimulation of heartbeat by a prosthesis will not lead to even more extremes in the near future, with the invasion of further procedures for speeding up biorhythms deemed too slow?

It is the Italian Futurists' dream actually come true nearly a century later: man's body fully fueled by technology, thanks to the miniaturization of "microbe machines" that are invisible—or as good as. There is one major difference, however, and that is in the order of magnitude of speed. It is no longer a matter of rivaling motor speed, as Marinetti had hoped, by making the individual's locomotive body equivalent to the locomotive or electric turbine, whose relative speeds have been exceeded. *It is now very much a matter of trying to rig up the human body to bring it up-to-date with the age of absolute speed of electromagnetic waves,* the real-time transceiver from now on ousting the super-high-powered motor capable of covering territory's real space as fast as possible.

We might remember that as soon as life began, the race has been an eliminating heat: eliminating for the predator able to catch up with its prey the fastest; eliminating equally for human societies unable to speed up their production and distribution processes. In this race, in this savage competition, the adversary (the animal that is too slow) is not the only one to be eliminated. Bits of one's own body also go. *One loses weight,* for example, to be in shape; one slims down to improve reflexes, synapses. Only, in so doing, one also eliminates natural territory by making it more "conductive," more streamlined. This is where INFRA-STRUCTURES such as the stadium, hippodrome, or aerodrome come in, *the real space of the place where the race is held suddenly becoming a product of the real time of a route.*

The "territorial" body is thus rigorously configured in the manner of the "animal" body of the runner or athlete; that is, it is wholly reconstituted by speed. Not long ago, this meant the *relative speed* of physical displacement. Now it means the *absolute speed* of microphysical transmission, finite speed, veritable LIGHT BARRIER—succeeding the barriers of sound and heat—in which the race, the essential competition, undergoes a kind of transmutation.

Since the standard of acceleration magnitude has reached the absolute limit of 180,000 miles per second (according to the law of relativity), *elimination will now be pursued right inside living matter,* this time by the reconstitution of vital dynamics, the phagocytosis of what is alive, of the subject's vitality itself. What gets stimulated will no longer be merely muscle building or joint elasticity through rhythmic exercise or steroids. Now the *nervous system will be stimulated,* the vitality of memory or the imagination, new mnemonic practices producing a restructuring of sensation.

At this stage in history, the eliminating game no longer eliminates weight in order to make the body trimmer and thereby more adapted to racing. It also alters vital rhythms and even goes as far as filling the gaps in the subject's intraorganic space by appending *substitute post organs.*

Marvin Minsky boasts about this kind of physiological reconstruction: *"This means that we might have all the space we need inside our skulls to implant systems and additional memories.* So you could gradually learn a bit more each year, add new kinds of perception, new modes of reasoning, new ways of thinking or imagining."[3]

Neuroscience's METADESIGN is thus no longer concerned with giving form to the structure or infrastructure of an industrial "object." It now wants to regenerate the impulses of the neurotransmitters of the living "subject," thereby achieving a sort of *cognitive ergonomics,* the latest kind of neuroleptic connection, which we could call behavioral INTRASTRUCTURE.

We might recall at this juncture a little-known fact to do with the decline in the primacy of the expanse of geographical space, and the subsequent, very recent, primacy of chronographic time's absence of duration. Bringing the body and its vital energy up to speed with the age of instant teletechnology means simultaneously abolishing the classic distinction between *internal* and *external*, while promoting a final type of centrality or, more exactly, hypercentrality— *that of time*, of some "present" if not "real" time—that has definitively overcome the distinction between periphery and center. Much as the antisleep pill suppresses alternation between wakefulness and reinvigorating sleep.

In days gone by, *being present meant being close*, being physically close to the other in face-to-face, vis-à-vis proximity. This made dialogue possible through the carrying of the voice and eye contact. But with the advent of *media proximity*, based on the properties of electromagnetic waves, the value of interlocutors' immediate coming together has suffered from interference, the sudden loss of distance rebounding on "being there," here and now. If it is true that, from now on, we can not only act at a distance, but even teleact at a distance—see, hear, speak, touch, and even smell at a distance[4]—then the unheard-of possibility arises of a sudden splitting of the subject's personality. This will not leave "body image"—the individual's SELF-PERCEPTION—intact for long. . . . Sooner or later, intimate perception of one's gravimetric mass will lose all concrete evidence, and the classic distinction between "inside" and "outside" will go out the window with it. The hypercenter of the *real time* (or, if you prefer, the living present) of one's own body—EGOCENTRATION—will then prevail over the center of the *real space* of one's own world—EXOCENTRATION—the essential notion of being and acting, here and now, losing all sense.

By way of illustration, here is what someone who has just undergone a liver transplant has to say: "It's amazing. What they told me, basically, is that when my liver became diseased, it got heavier, like a deadweight. Afterward, when the graft finally took, I was frightened of losing the new liver. I was afraid it would come away from my insides. I was like a pregnant woman in the final month, trying to avoid any sudden movement so as not to give birth prematurely."

We die in detail, the anatomist, Xavier Bichat, explained. . . . *But what about living? Can we live in detail?* With a shattered sense of unity and thus of self-perceptive identity? When the patient openly declares that "something inside is falling" like a deadweight (his diseased liver), or like a foreign body not sufficiently integrated with his internal organs (the grafted liver), he is pointing to the existence of a kind of vital gravity, of weightiness of the body proper's insides, that characterizes both the disease and its remedy, the transplant, at once. I refer to intraorganic gravitation, which effectively doubles the external gravity of the living body in the middle of its own world, at the center of the geographical expanse of one planet among others, all equally subject to universal attraction. . . . The surgeon René Leriche claimed, "*Silence means your organs are healthy.*" In effect, our patient's sensation of intraorganic dislocation operates *a curious confusion between the world in which we move around at the risk of falling, and the world which moves around in us, regardless of us.* A world with a certain physiological integrity whose discretion, until now, guaranteed a peaceful life.

We are back at Nietzsche's hype. Speaking about ZARATHUSTRA, himself seen as a "type," Nietzsche says, "To understand this type, one must first be clear about his fundamental physiological condition: *this is what I call great health.* . . . Being new, nameless, self-evident, we premature births of an as-yet-unproven future, we need new means to a new end—*namely, a new health,* stronger, more seasoned, tougher, more audacious, and gayer than any previous health."[5]

With such a reworking of bodily "health," if not of the body itself, it is important to have a different kind of nutrition. According to the philosopher, the man of the future will need "above all else: GREAT HEALTH—*that one does not merely have but also acquires continually, and must acquire because one gives it up again and again, and must give it up.*"[6] We all know what he goes on to say: how we need men "who are healthier than one likes to permit us, dangerously healthy"; men, supermen rather, whose reward ought to be "an as-yet-undiscovered country whose boundaries nobody has yet surveyed, *something beyond all the lands and nooks of the ideal so far.*"[7]

Alas, such a resplendent beyond has recently become the simple within of all lands, of our own world's territorial boundaries. Despite the grand illusion of the so-called conquest of space, the implementation of absolute speed, the relativization of all magnitudes and regression to the infinitesimal. From now on there is no future in long journeys—not even intergalactic ones. The loss of the terrestrial horizon of our world proper is the loss of all measure. Outside planet EARTH, nothing is "big" or far away; *perspective* exists only in intrusion, in intraorganic introspection, physiological corporality suddenly becoming the final yardstick of the measurement of movement. Only, of *movement on-the-spot,* right inside an animal body that has become the ultimate planet.

Beyond the boundaries of our biosphere, there are indeed no *dimensions* worthy of the name: no more height, breadth, or depth, no yesterday and no tomorrow, only light-years. Less a type of "time," a measure of duration, than a cosmic disproportion: that of the speed of light, absolute speed and ultimate limit, whence the optical illusion of the dilation of a supposedly *expanding* universe.[8]

From Fred Astaire to Michael Jackson, hyperactive man has plenty of ancestors, especially among the dancers dear to Nietzsche, actors and contortionists, people whose bodies have gradually become instruments. But the most recent specimen would have to be an Australian, Stelios Arcadiou, better known as Stelarc. When asked just exactly what he is up to on stage, Stelarc answers, "*I'm trying to extend the body's capabilities through technology.* For instance, I use medical techniques, sound systems, a robot hand [the Third Hand] and an artificial arm [the Ambidextrous Arm]. There are four kinds of movement in my performances: the improvised movement of the body, the movement of the robot hand, which is controlled by sensors in my stomach and leg muscles, the programmed movement of the artificial arm, and the movement of my left arm when it's involuntarily agitated by an electric current. It's the interaction of these voluntary, involuntary, and computerized movements that I find interesting."[9]

Adept at the perfect symbiosis of the human and the technological, Stelarc has this to say about whether or not he is a choreographer: "I don't have any training in music or choreography, but I can, for example, *amplify body sounds and signals like brain waves, blood flow, or muscle movement.* This is both a physical experience and an artistic expression at the same time."

Claiming to be a survivor of the age of human physiology, as well as of philosophy, Stelarc goes on to explain, "As I've been performing, I've begun to ask myself about THE DESIGN OF THE HUMAN BODY. The more work I do, the more I believe the human body is obsolete!

"Technology today is more precise and more powerful than the human body. *We're no longer limited in space to the biosphere.* . . . We're heading for extraterrestrial space, but our body is only designed for this biosphere."

Taking up Nietzsche's theme, the artist goes on to declare that "deconstruction" should apply not only to language, that medium of communication par excellence, but also to human physiology, the beginning and end of our perception of the world: "*The ultimate limit of philosophy is the limit of physiology,* of our feeble organic capabilities, our pan-aesthetic vision of the world. . . . I believe that evolution in fact ends with the technological invasion of the body."

Bristling with electrodes and antennae and sporting two *laser eyes,* our willing mutant takes the analogy with teleoperator robotics to its logical conclusion: the man lurks inside the android. But this is a pretty drastic conversion, for it achieves exactly the opposite of what Stelarc is hoping: "Today, technology has stuck to us like glue. *It's about to become a component of our bodies,* from watches to artificial hearts. For me, this represents the end of Darwinian evolution as some organic development over millions of years through natural selection. Now, with nanotechnology, man can swallow technology. So we need to see the body as a 'structure.' *It is only by modifying the body's architecture that we'll be able to reshape our consciousness of the world.*"

Keen to see our body proper burst out of its biological envelope, Stelarc moves on to the fallen-angels theme: "Once the body is tackled by the precision and power of technology, once it is propelled beyond Earth's atmosphere, we won't be talking about 'language' anymore; we'll be talking about 'structure,' including body structure, physiology."

When asked whether he is not *just inventing the Eve of the future,* Stelarc retorts, "It's not that simple! For me, in the beginning was not the Word! I don't envisage adapting space to our bodies, but, on the contrary, remodeling our bodies. So the question is: *how do we shape a panplanetary human physiology?*"

Anxious finally to get down to this BODY, this MAN-PLANET, say, who will be liberated from Earth's attraction, the categorical imperative of a human type that will have become postevolutionary, Stelarc continues, "In other words, we must ask the question: how do we reshape the human body so that it can cope with varied conditions in atmosphere, gravity, and electromagnetic fields?"

Ranting on the theme of intergalactic travel the way astronauts typically do, Stelarc further explains that, since future expeditions will be measured in light-years, it will be possible to prolong life, not in some Faustian search for immortality, but in the interests of a *necessary extension of extraterrestrial intelligence.*

Once again, the exotic desire for some "great out-of-this-world voyage" is merely an alibi for the technical intrusion into an inner world, that of our viscera: "*We'll soon be able to empty out the human body and replace malfunctioning organs through new technologies!* What would happen, for instance, if we were able to acquire a new skin capable of simultaneously breathing and achieving photosynthesis, transforming sunlight into food? If we were equipped with that kind of skin, we would no longer need a mouth to chew with, or an esophagus to swallow, or a stomach to digest, or lungs to breathe."

You will note that Marvin Minsky's idea of a few years ago of some sort of phagocytosis of internal space has already caught on. It follows from this that the far horizon finds itself replaced by a substitute horizon: the substance of our gravimetric mass expands in the manner of the mass of the cosmos, giving way to a new form of postindustrial and, especially, "postevolutionary," rigging out of the living being. *"The new perspective is that the body can be colonized by miniaturized synthetic organisms, whereas previously, technology was content to surround the body, to protect it from the outside."*

It is clear from this that the project of colonization—of endocolonization—is no longer one of surrounding the patient's body with its attentions. It now entails transforming the body into "primary material," making a laboratory rat of hyperactive man in the process. Just listen to the crescendo of Stelarc's symptomatic rave. "Instruments have always been outside the human body. But now technology is no longer exploding a long way away from the body, it's imploding inside the body. This is highly significant; it is perhaps the single most important event in our history: *we no longer need to send technology to other planets, we can land it in our own bodies!*"[10]

As you can see, the conversion is complete. Under the guise of "extraterrestrial" liberation, the technosciences are getting their teeth into a weightless *man-planet* whom nothing can now really protect, neither ethics nor biopolitical morality. Instead of escaping from our natural biosphere, we will colonize an infinitely more accessible planet—as so often in the past—that of a body-without-a-soul, a profane body, on behalf of a science-without-a-conscience that has never ceased to profane the space of the body of animals and slaves, the colonized of former empires. We have never, in fact, dominated geophysical expanse without controlling, increasingly tightly, the substance, the microphysical core of the subject being: from the domestication of other species to the rhythmic training of the soldier or servant, the alienation of the production worker, force-feeding sports champions anabolic steroids. All of these examples illustrate this latest project, of which our Australian is clearly not the instigator, but rather a victim, a willing victim, as so often the case with the servant corrupted by the master. At a time when there is talk of *ethnic cleansing* in Europe, the auditing of the evacuated living being's viscera is a timely reminder of the dangers of neuroscience's endogenous tyranny, of a *cognitive ergonomics* already at work on the latest in HUMAN DESIGN, the training of conditioned reflexes, the METADESIGN of our conceptual and perceptual faculties. With the latter, the reign of the computer will at last catch up with the patient's body, underneath his clothes, his uniform, thereby achieving a new type of "underclothing" in which the smartening up of our nervous system will supersede the DESIGN of the consumer object of the waning industrial age.

Having arrived at this particular point in the history of science and technology, the issue of the evolution of living things in Darwin's terms takes on a different significance—especially now that the theory of evolution is being challenged not only through the convergence of various religious and philosophical interpretations, but also by apologists of evolutionary science such as Professor Louis Thaler of Montpellier University. "It seems to me beyond question that man is today evolving under the influence of what I would call a *relaxation of the selection process.* This phenomenon is one of the effects of progress, especially in medicine."[11]

Taking up Stelarc's argument about the decline of Darwinism once technology can invade man's body with its prostheses, Professor Thaler continues, "Good eyesight is a *survival factor* among those tribes that are still hunters and gatherers, and so is good hearing. This is clearly not the case for modern man, who can correct such faults with glasses or hearing aids."

Coming back later to the importance of genetic mutation, Thaler further specifies, "*Evolution is based on mutations.* These fruits of chance are statistically more often a disadvantage, a handicap; the number of 'good' mutations that get through is accordingly very small. Until now, in conditions where natural selection has been a strong pressure, these always ended up dominating 'bad' mutations. Today this is no longer the case. Mutations are asserting themselves more and more insistently."

Which is where the idea of some kind of veiled "chronic fatigue" comes in, of a significant relaxation of selective pressure in an artificial environment in which the "technosphere" prevails over the "biosphere."

It is really quite something now to be witnessing the renunciation of the doctrine of selective power by the very people who set themselves up as apostles of evolutionary science and thereby of the survival of the fittest.

What lies behind such materialist pessimism? "The relaxation of the process of natural selection allows us to predict an accumulation of genetic defects over the generations and thus a human population fitted with a *growing number of prostheses*—and blowing out the cost of health care."

One might note in passing that this thesis has been effectively corroborated by the experts, who predict that in the year 2000, half of all surgical operations performed will involve transplants and the installation of prostheses.

"Saving premature babies in our maternity wards," Louis Thaler goes on to argue, "will tend to introduce mutations into the population that once would have tended to be eliminated. With the present data on evolution, *we can thus predict a relative long-term degeneration of the human species*. Relative, because this process of 'nonselection' produces little change in the average characteristics of the human population. What it involves in particular is a greater disparity between features within a certain framework: *what enables the species to achieve equilibrium with its environment*."

We are thus seeing a kind of convergence between the concept of a breakdown in "natural" selection and that of "ecological" imbalance, such an imbalance attacking not only the human habitat—the quality of the substances that make up our natural surroundings—but also the mechanism regulating the relationship between "our body proper" and "our world proper." The director of Montpellier's Sciences of Evolution Institute also claims that *"natural selection is primarily a stabilizing factor and only secondarily a motor for evolution.* It ends in the elimination of specimens different from the norm. With the relaxation of natural selection that medicine produces—along with development of the technosphere—this mechanism becomes less important, paving the way for more and more mutations and thus genetic malformations."

Well aware of how such a discourse might chime and of the risk of being mistaken for a eugenicist, Professor Thaler clarifies, "I must emphasize that this predictable 'relative degeneration' is only discernable in the physical realm. It has no bearing on the mental except in pathological cases. The Nazis also spoke of degeneration and campaigned for a form of saving eugenics, arguing the existence of an intellectually and physically superior race, something that obviously has no scientific basis."

Even if such a remark is indispensable in avoiding some kind of slur or racist misinterpretation, the issue of Darwinism's having become old hat remains. If the "superman" of tomorrow is indeed the *superequipped, able-bodied person* controlling the environment without having to stir a limb, in the manner of the *disabled person equipped* with prostheses who can already act and get around without much call on muscle power, then evolution will have entered a TECHNOSCIENTIFIC phase. This is an eventuality our natural selection expert evidently fails to mention, even though his declaration of insolvency suddenly reintroduces the possibility, if not of a "superior race," then at least of a "species equipped in superior fashion." This is, after all, merely the accomplishment of what politicians have been calling economic and social progress ever since industry in the West began to flourish. In discussing evolution, even if it is most important to distinguish between the "physiological" and the "social" to avoid any eugenic drift, the problem of the *technological* cannot be separated from the *sociological,* once we are confronted by the premises of a kind of TECHNICAL FUNDAMENTALISM: the prospective reconstruction of the human body, either by adding superficial prostheses, or intraorganically intruding these inside our very organs, which is what the nanotechnology of living organisms—the BIOTECHNOLOGY of the future—proposes.

So if the natural environment—the biosphere—exerts pressures that would lead to natural selection according to Darwin, it may also be that the artificial environment—the technosphere—exerts pressures too, the inertia of the sedentary urbanite not being without effect.

The issue of controlling the environment by means of interactive prostheses that function in real time does not essentially involve development of an already devalued geographical and territorial body. It involves developing, equipping man's animal body by means of intrastructures of which the pacemaker is and will long remain the perfect emblem because it acts on the rhythm, on the vital energy of the living being.[12]

The question of freedom is thus central to the problematic of technoscience and of neuroscience equally. To what extent can the individual avoid sensory confusion? To what extent will he still be able to keep his distance when faced with the sudden hyperstimulation of his senses? What new kind of dependency or addiction will be produced in the near future? Will they involve possession or dispossession? The question remains entirely open, though we can at least assume that design will play a big role—the METADE-SIGN of morals and behavior—since humanity will thus be exposed to experiment, indeed to life-size experimentation with a veritable METAPHYSICAL body, a METABODY independent of surrounding conditions, to the extent that *real space*—the expanse of our own world as well as, equally, the density of our own body—will gradually fade into the background as *real time* nanotechnological impulses and hyperstimulation take over from vital rhythms.

A few further questions remain. Does the proclaimed degeneration in evolution take us from natural selection to a kind of *artificial* selection, the product of technoscientific progress whereby the *physical body* of pedestrian man (Kierkegaard) will gradually lose its usefulness and bow out as a *truly metaphysical body* capable of replacing it emerges?

Haven't we already seen, with last century's boom in machine tools, for example, the beginnings of a similar substitution of the technical for the muscular effort of the worker?

Aren't we now about to see the "technical" unemployment of the common laborer of the erstwhile industrial firm replaced by a kind of compulsory unemployment of certain vital organs considered obsolete and whose energy output will be seen to be totally inadequate?

Following the trashing of the history of the "proletariat," surely we will soon see human physiology turfed out and wrecked, once it is considered irretrievably obsolete compared to the prowess of intraorganic nanotechnologies. Faced with the demands of an increasingly artificial terrestrial environment and the disastrous consequences of a criminal level of pollution that will make the old "outdoor life" largely out of bounds, will we not then see a new type of FUNDAMENTALISM emerge, one no longer associated with the trust in God of traditional beliefs, but with the worship, the "technocult," of a perverted science? This would be a veritable TECHNOSCIENTIFIC FUNDAMENTALISM that will do as much damage as any religious fanaticism. The will to power of a science without a conscience will pave the way for a kind of intolerance yet unimaginable today precisely insofar as it will not simply attack certain peculiarities of the species, like sex, race, or religion. It will attack what is alive, "natural" vitality finally being eliminated by the quasi-messianic coming of wholly *hyperactivated* man.

If this were to happen, we would then see a reversal, the inversion of Nietzsche's logic. Over to Nietzsche: "When the least organ in an organism fails, however slightly, to enforce with complete self-assurance its self-preservation, its 'egoism,' restitution of its *energies,* the whole degenerates. The physiologist demands excision of the degenerating part; *he denies all solidarity with what degenerates; he is worlds removed from pity for it.* But the priest desires precisely the degeneration of the whole, of humanity: for that reason, he conserves what degenerates."[13]

What can you say when it is "science" itself that announces the degeneration of human evolution? Except that science in turn is taking on the role of a new kind of "priesthood" in the absence of a new form of *sanctity;* one which would preside over the birth of a new form of *health,* for a new body, a METABODY composed of surrogate organs more efficient than the ones our natural physiology provides.

At the end of *Ecce Homo,* Nietzsche concludes, "Finally —and this is what is most terrible of all—the concept of the good man signifies that one sides with all that is weak, sick, with failure, suffering of itself—all that ought to perish. *The law of selection is thwarted*—an ideal is fabricated out of opposing the proud and well-turned-out human being who says Yes, who is sure of the future, who guarantees the future—and he is now called evil . . . And all this was believed, as morality!"[14]

When the *law of natural selection* is no longer thwarted by faith in the transcendence of being alone, but by some *law of artificial selection*—the sudden advent, beyond GOOD and EVIL, of a TECHNICAL FUNDAMENTALISM, as opposed to the old MYSTICAL kind—what is left of the "great health" of Nietzsche's superseded man? The imminent production of biotechnological SUPERVITALITY will surely undermine the very foundation of the philosophy of the "superman."

The question of what will happen to DESIGN, or more precisely, to "postindustrial" METADESIGN, finds its basis here—I would go so far as to say its METAPHYSICAL basis. It is just a step from last century's evolutionary superman to the hyperactive, postevolutionary man of the coming century, just one more step into the gloom of postscientific obscurantism.

"Man is progressing from the species to the superspecies," according to Nietzsche. In the realm of the living, the live, aren't we now seeing progress in health? Aren't sports practices a sure index of this "postmodern" attempt to speed up the living, the animate, the way the inanimate, the machine, has always been made to go faster?

We might answer these questions in the affirmative, as far as an increase in longevity goes. For about a hundred years, the "quantitative" has been effectively improved and human life expectancy has shot up from about fifty to seventy years and over—for man in so-called advanced countries. Hence the surreptitious return of eugenics in the guise of a concern for public health. As Pierre-André Taguieff says, denouncing the increasingly Mephistophelian nature of genetic research, *"There is now a demand for eugenics based on the image of a universal health horizon."*[15]

We need to take a closer look at the recent evolution of this new brand of *public health ideology,* an ideology that is no longer particularly interested in maintaining public health so much as in continually improving it. The goal is no longer just to *live better,* comfortably consuming goods and medicine; one must now *live more acutely*, one must build up the nervous intensity of being alive by ingesting biotechnological products whose role is thus to make up for food and other more or less stimulating chemical substances.

To really be in "good health," will we soon have to be constantly doped, artificially overstimulated, like top athletes or enthusiasts of extremist sports?

Remember, for the biologist, *excitability is the fundamental property of living tissue*. Tomorrow, will hyperexcitability become one of the fundamental properties *of the living person*, for the physiologist? If to be is to be excited, then *to be alive is to be speed*, a metabolic speed that technology is compelled to increase and improve, the way it has done with animal species.

Following the ravages of *"the law of least action,"* which has always restricted man's muscular activity in the name of economizing physical effort—and thereby of extending comfort to the panoply of ordinary movements—we are now seeing a sort of *energy transmutation* in human behavior. Rendered passive, if not inert, by the employment of various prostheses of transport and instantaneous transmission, man will no longer feel the need to economize physical effort. Hence the emergence of a new law entailing the opposite; this time it will be a matter of treating the living being like a motor, *a machine that needs to be constantly revved up.*

The former law of least action of the age of exploitation of geophysical space—contemporaneous with progress in transport and broadcasting—will find itself saddled with another law, one better adapted to the age of the micro-physical transplant revolution. This law will aim to *promote increasing acceleration of the reflexes and stimuli of the animate being.*

We might again recall that the progress of contemporary technoscience is itself conditioned by the need to econo-mize the efforts of the individual subject to Earth's gravity and therefore to the nervous and muscular fatigue resulting from his own mass and physiological density.

Having recently achieved the implementation of abso-lute speed and thereby freeing people from the traditional conditions of existence, remote-control teletechnology will not be content with further economizing fatigue due to physical exertion. It will be driven to try to get rid of the dissatisfaction and frustration that result from the grow-ing passivity and inertia of the individual dispossessed of immediate physical activity. Whence the desire *to over-stimulate* the patient's organism at the same time as *tran-quilizing;* in other words, to "program" the very intensity of the patient's nervous and intellectual activities just as the motor function of a machine is now already pro-grammed.

Merce Cunningham says apropos, "Electronic music has changed everything for me and for dance. Until now, the beat of the music forced the dancer to count. Rhythm was something physical, muscular. *But electronic music affects your nerves, not your muscles. It's difficult to count elec-tricity!*"[16]

But let's get back to environmental control—in other words, to the loss of the classic distinction between "inside" and "outside," this loss being connected to the diminished importance of the expanse of real space as opposed to real time and its practical lack of duration.

In the face of what is now known as an "open system," it helps to recall the third and final state of matter, that is, the *concept of information* nowadays outstripping the notions of mass and energy.

During the Second World War, engineers at Bell Corporation discovered an *observable physical property* whose use ensured improved transmission. They called it INFORMATION. . . . Norbert Wiener, the father of cybernetics, Immediately defined this in terms of what it was not. *"Information is not mass, or energy; information is information."* It is thus the third fundamental dimension of matter. Later, much later, Gregory Bateson, who was one of the first to think of information as a general process, added that *"Information is a difference that makes a difference."*[17]

But the redundancy is the same, traditional notions of *entrance* and *exit* losing their spatial and environmental connotation and becoming *"the difference difference,"* the IN and OUT of logical ports, the o and 1 of computer science.

After this, the logic of differentiation is reduced to its LOGISTICS, a CYBERNETIC logistics that will achieve that takeover by force without which NO INFORMATION worthy of the name can exist, since this is never anything more than *the effect of a fact,* the reflection of some power relationship.

"Surprise me!" Diaghilev used to say to his dancers. We know what he means. If *"the law of stimulation"* from now on takes over from the law of least action, we have come full circle: it is no longer a matter of maintaining health by reducing fatigue and effort; it is now a matter of amplifying the subject's vitality through the impulses of information biotechnologies.

"Great health" is thus no longer a GIFT, the gift of our organs' silence. It is a HORIZON, a perspective that can be attained thanks to LIVE technologies' feats of acceleration. Brave new world not unrelated to the aspirations of mystics toward some future transfiguration of humanity. *"He treated his body as though it were his soul,"* Rainer Maria Rilke writes in a short story about a pantheist attempt at fusion with nature . . . .

But this final "perspective," based on the image of a horizon of great health for all, rests on the primacy of real time over the real space of the body, or, if you like, on the abolition of the importance of the classic intervals of "space" and "time," to the sole advantage of the third interval: the interface of the "light-speed" type.

Whence the decline already discussed in the usual notions of internal and external, INSIDE and OUTSIDE, which until now subtended the difference between the living being and its environment.

This makes more sense of the recent devaluation and subtle discrediting of the notion of *whole dimension,* since critical space currently secretes an infinite number of fractal, deconstructive subdivisions that end up eliminating the very idea of environment. . . . The architect Le Corbusier held that *outside is always inside!* For the specialists of neuroscience, *inside is always outside* from now on! Internal space lies open like a town about to be destroyed by invaders.

Lawyer Bernard Edelman writes:

> Thanks to scientific progress, we have become radically contingent. Now there is nothing from a scientific point of view that grounds us to the land, that essentially attaches us to our species. It's in this context that we need to understand the extraordinary triumph of biomedicine—a triumph echoed, incidentally, by the market economy. This success has caught us completely unaware, *for we have neutralized our markers as creatures of "the soil" as well as our markers as a "species."*[18]

In such exotic conditions, how can we hope to preserve for long the self-perceptual distinction between the whole body, *here and now,* and that of the world, between an individual's vitality and the particular vivacity of his organs, or rather, his "organoids"?

Will Earth soon become humanity's phantom limb?

If fractalization no longer solely affects extension, the ideal dimensions of geometry, but first and foremost the intensity of the living being's nerve influx and biorhythms, *how do we locate ourselves?* As you will have remarked, the problem for "bioethics" is the carving up of the body's space. But at the philosophical level, there is also the problem of duration, in other words, of the living body's particular temporality.

On one hand, there is the question of the dismemberment of the body and thus of a possible, lucrative "organ trade."[19] On the other is the question of CYBERNETIC programming of vital rhythms, as though the *substitute servicing* of spare parts in mechanics might be applied to the human organism: *xenotransplants* and *technotransplants* equally allowing the body's vital functions to be improved or damage caused by disease to this or that organ to be repaired. Some people are already eriously pondering the *interchangeability of human beings* (or their organs) and even the possibility of *body substitutability*.

In his introduction to an anthology of essays on bioethics and citizenship, Alain Caillé writes:

> The common ground in this debate is utilitarianism, if we understand by the term "utilitarianism" the doctrine that acknowledges the greatest happiness of the greatest number as sole criterion of justice and morality. Certainly, an argument that justifies a priori unlimited economic and technological expansion is unanswerable. *Who could object to the resultant increase in pleasure and reduction of suffering?* The only drawback of such an irrefutable doctrine is that, in the name of maximizing an individual's pleasure and minimizing their pain, it runs the real risk of sapping what makes existence livable.[20]

We are back at the Nietzschean myth of GREAT HEALTH and, with it, the myth of the new eugenics, a "eugenics" that would extend the pleasure principle and so-called gratification handed down from the age of the consumer society. Only this time it would be aimed at a sort of *perpetual stimulation,* as though the law of least effort until now governing technoscientific progress no longer made any sense. This, at the very moment that *postindustrial automation* is finally achieving perfect economization of muscular effort, along with the dismissal, the structural unemployment, of pedestrian man, so dear to Kierkegaard, in favor of digital transfer machines. . . . The passivity of individuals made useless, hence supernumery, becoming a social menace because of the strong component of boredom and discontent.

"The less human strength is occupied, the more it tends to excess," you will recall Balzac's saying in his *Treaty on Modern Stimulants.* It is clear from this that we cannot separate the new eugenics from the *general mobilization of affects,* the mobilization of the emotions. This process goes through an organism "motorization" phase in which the individual suddenly becomes the packaging, the hood over the engine of micromachines capable of transplanting life and transfusing its impulses with the help of computer software.

In the *Futurist Manifesto* of 1910, Marinetti trumpeted, "*With us begins the reign of uprooted man,* of multiple man who gets tangled up in iron and feeds on electricity. *Let's make way for the imminent and inevitable identification of man with the motor.*"

Eighty years later, we have brought this off with the emergence and mass production of ORGANOIDS originating in biotechnological research. Similarly, scientists are not content simply to diminish para- or tetraplegics' disabilities by means of external prostheses—wheelchairs or motorized chairs for the seriously disabled. Recently, they have been working on an *internal prosthesis* using electrodes implanted in the patient's legs and controlled by a microcomputer. This electronic system would be called on to provide stimulation of defective muscles that normally comes from the spinal cord.[21] Pedestrian man thus becomes *electromobile man* in the manner of the electric car. . . .

Marinetti's manifesto also proposes, *"Let's combine forces with mechanical engineering to destroy the old poetry of distance."* This has now happened too. If the greatest geographical distances are nothing now thanks to the progress of hypersonic speed, the more minute layers protecting the living organism's insides have become less than nothing in the face of the implementation of the absolute speed of electronic impulses. As though the *speed limit* of electromagnetic waves had once and for all overtaken the imperceptible limit of cutaneous tissue.

From now on, the beings and things that surround us are merely FIELDS and the real a single NETWORK—only, a CYBERNETIC network since everything is exclusively internal to the "field."

In order to approach in any way, finally, *the reality of the facts,* we clearly must have another look at solids, forms, and forces . . . the putting into waves of the real tending to generalize—with the primacy of the notion of information over those of mass and energy—*that takeover by force* that consists of undermining the concrete nature of the event and promoting its sole "communication."

So after the different forms of pollution resulting from *regional industrial development,* we are seeing the beginnings of a new form of pollution caused by the *control of the global environment* by postindustrial technologies that exhaust the space-time intervals that once organized the world.

"The greater the increase in mobility, the greater the control," a nineteenth-century specialist in rail BLOCK SYSTEMS asserted. But at the time, "mobilization" was all that was involved. The sudden "motorization of the living being" had not yet occurred. It is this that we are victims of today. With excess transmission speed, *control becomes the environment itself.*

When the limited transport revolution gives way to the general spread of the instantaneous transmission revolution, information theory—COMPUTER SCIENCE—takes over from the physical, we might as well say, the astrophysical! Fusion is achieved, confusion total: INFORMATION is reality's only "relief," its only "volume"; in the age of synthetic images and sound, we might say, its "high definition." Alongside *potential energy* and *kinetic energy,* we now have a third form of energy, *information energy.* Following the three phases of displacement—departure, journey, arrival—and after the demise of the "journey," suddenly it is "departure" that we have lost. From now on, *everything arrives* without our having to leave. But what "arrives" is already no longer a stopover or the end of the trip; it is merely information, *information-world,* no, *information-universe!* The reign of the generalized arrival from then on combines with the generalization of *real-time* information. And so everything rushes at man, man-the-target is assailed on all sides, and our only salvation now is to be found in illusion, in flight from the reality of the moment, from the loss of free will whose advent Pascal evoked when he wrote, "Our senses cannot perceive extremes. Too much noise deafens us, too much light dazzles. . . . Extreme qualities are our enemies. We no longer feel anything; we suffer."

THE ART OF
THE MOTOR

The computer and special software together
constitute what is known in the
Virtual Reality trade as
the "reality engine."

HOWARD RHEINGOLD

IT WAS ONLY A SKIP and a jump from social Darwinism to *biotechnological cybernetics*. The jump was easily taken in the Second World War, by the very people who victoriously opposed the biocracy of a National Socialist State that based its political legitimacy on the utopia of a redemptive eugenics. *Total mobilization and motorization* have always been two sides of the same coin in the race for biological and technological supremacy.

During this period when the various principles of the same massive attack on living beings were being worked out—at Auschwitz as at Hiroshima—Claude Shannon (1938) and Norbert Wiener (1948) independently collaborated on defining a trend that was to take us from the earlier BIOCRACY to a veritable TELECRACY designed to construct the "common collective conscience" that Stephan

Zweig felt humanity's progress would be based on and that, in the end, turns out to be merely the creation of a social cybernetics based on the cult of information.[1]

It is strange the way everyone remembers Charlie Chaplin in his role as the tragicomic dictator, yet not many remember the worker in *Modern Times,* tormented by his assembly-line job, force-fed by an *automatic feeder,* even though we march today to the beat of postindustrial automation, thanks to the computing capabilities of "transfer machines" . . .

A worker in the textile industry in western France says, "I make the same movement six hundred times an hour. With the old machines, you could have a bit of a break. Now, it's the computer that controls the assembly line and sets the pace."

With this level of hyperproductivity, in which a person can no longer keep up with the racing of his digital command tools, we are seeing a new epidemic, following the outbreak of stress. Repetitive Strain Injury, or RSI—acute inflammation of the bones and joints—is a new professional disease. It can lead to long-term paralysis of the employee's hands.

The common origin of *biopolitical* conditioning in Germany and *telepolitical* enslavement in the Anglo-Saxon world has been too soon forgotten. Today we are reduced to patting ourselves on the back over "technological progress" responsible not only for structural unemployment and the closing down of masses of factories and businesses, but, more especially, for the impasse that's looming on the

horizon.[2] As Maurice Merleau-Ponty pointed out in his last
summer of 1960, "Functional thought has become a sort of
absolutely artificial construct that has human creation de-
riving from a natural process of information, but this is itself modeled on the man-made machine."[3]

The war of total mobilization was obviously well worth
winning against Nazism with its racial and eugenic goals,
but it was also the main catalyst in the development of a
purely statistical notion of INFORMATION due to the strategic necessities of intelligence,[4] and thus led to the gradual
spread of a SOCIOPOLITICAL CYBERNETICS that tends to
eliminate not only the weak, but also the component of free
will in human work, promoting, as we have seen, so-called
"interactive user-friendliness." This is just a metaphor for
the subtle enslavement of the human being to "intelligent"
machines; a programmed symbiosis of man and computer
in which assistance and the much trumpeted "dialogue between man and the machine" scarcely conceal the premises: not of an avowed racial discrimination this time so
much as of the total, unavowed disqualification of the human in favor of the definitive instrumental conditioning of
the individual.

According to John von Neumann, his work, *The Computer and the Brain* (1958), involves " . . . an approach toward the understanding of the nervous system from the
mathematician's point of view. . . . The 'mathematician's
point of view,' as I would like to have it understood in this
context, carries a distribution of emphases that differs
from the usual one: apart from the stress on the general

mathematical techniques, the logical and the statistical aspects will be in the foreground. *Furthermore, logic and statistics should be primarily, although not exclusively, viewed as the basic tools of 'information theory.'* Also, that body of experience which has grown up around the planning, evaluating, and coding of complicated logical and mathematical automata will be the focus of much of this information theory."[5]

The founding influence of statistics on contemporary functional thought has already been noted in the growth of mass societies and totalitarian Marxist systems. But, curiously, the innovatory role of statistics in fine-tuning the theory of *cybernetic domination* has been neglected—despite what Norbert Wiener, for instance, had to say when, just after the war, admittedly a little late, he warned of the dangers of the MILITARY-COMMUNICATIONS COMPLEX. he automatic or *servomotor* appliance and what is called artificial or *motor-brain* intelligence were soon confused in people's minds! The 1950s, in any case, deserve much closer historical analysis, insofar as they were the direct product of the military-industrial strategy that had been directed against Nazi Germany. Once the urgency of world war abated, the scientific community that had centered on Bletchley Park to fight Hitler then found itself tackling futuristic themes that were sometimes frankly utopian such as the idea, as old as Descartes and especially La Mettrie, of identifying the human brain with the components of a computer. A synthesis of data theory, game theory, signal theory, and neurobiology, the emergent cybernetics would thus at-

tempt to simulate the organization of the living being on IN-
TELLIGENT MACHINES, after the title of the book by Alan Turing, published in 1947. The combination of cybernetics
and *real-time* telecommunication technology would soon
enable the gap still separating information *logic* and its *logistics* to be closed. The opportunity came at the end of the
1950s with the U.S. antiair defense project. With the aim of
ensuring radar cover of North America, the U.S. Air Force
called upon the Lincoln Laboratory at MIT to set up a research unit and come up with an advance warning system as
quickly as possible: the SAGE Network (Semi-Automatic
Ground Environment). The Lexington laboratory that had
already built the WHIRLWIND, the first operational computer functioning in real time, then got down to the job of
perfecting a computerized ground defense network to protect America, a gigantic spiderweb whose objective was to
ensure control of an entire continent.

Numerous innovations in computer technology were
spin-offs of the effective installation of this warning system, which used a real-time radar network for the very first
time. One example we might cite is the notion of *time-shar-
ing,* the coupling of the computer and the telephone that
would give rise to TELEMATICS, computer simulation and
even the beginnings of digital imagery. . . . [6] In its way, the
SAGE system opened the door to the world of virtual reality, that otherworld made necessary by the delivery speed
of nuclear weapons.

Since the *real* environment—urban and rural space—
could no longer escape the influence of electromagnetic

networks, the possibility of reconditioning it by a *virtual,* fundamentally cybernetic environment became a reality. As a result, the incredible opportunity even arose of adding an extra, though simulated, dimension to the normal dimensions of human activity: computer-generated CYBERSPACE thereafter introducing a "fractional" dimension alongside the "whole" dimensions of our customary milieu.

But another aspect of this theoretical mutation deserves our attention: information's *energetic* side. Immediately after the war, you will recall, MATTER, until then considered in terms of MASS and ENERGY, was rounded off by the addition of the notion of INFORMATION. But, as relativity teaches, if the usual notions of mass and energy are distinct but equivalent—$E=mc^2$—we then had to try to capture the relationship between information and energy.

From the 1950s onward, then, it became a question of assimilating "information" with "energy," a form of energy as yet unknown in physics. After *latent* (potential) energy and actual (kinetic) energy, the possibility of *data* (cybernetic) energy arose. Initially, with management data processing, it was the economic aspect of energy that prevailed as a key factor in industrial production. But with the subsequent emergence of *computerized simulation* and the boom in telecommunications, evidently promoting TELE-ACTION, information comes to the fore as an entirely separate form of energy: *sound and image* energy, the energy of long-distance touch and contact. By saving on physical displacement, teleoperator technology suddenly looked like a serious rival to transport energy. The implementation of absolute speed in signal transmission eliminated the relative speed of the circulation of products, goods, and people, enabling huge strides in automatic traffic regulation due to various servocontrol processes. Information suddenly looked like the same thing as its limit speed.

This telematic fusion/confusion of energy and *live* information ended up leading to the absolute equivalence of electronics and computer science, as though the energy of electricity had slyly turned into *computer energy*.

To understand this veritable sleight of hand better, though, we need to go back a few years to 1942, when the "behavioral methodology" was elaborated by advocates Norbert Wiener, cardiologist Arturo Rosenblueth, and Julian Bigelow, a young engineer. "The method consisted of privileging BEHAVIOR in studying whatever kind of phenomenon, whether natural or artificial. In other words, the changes the phenomenon undergoes due to its relationship with its environment. For a long time the object of mathematics had been the RELATIONSHIP between various phenomena, but the novelty of the behavioral method consisted in its virtually universal application and its radical character: *there was no reality other than that constituted by the relationships between phenomena.* In privileging observation of the behavior of objects independently of the physical nature of the organs composing them, the new method made it possible to compare any 'objects' whatsoever—in particular, man and the machine. The traditional distinction among beings according to whether they belonged to the categories of mineral, vegetable, animal, or human thus yielded to a comparison that was oblivious to matter but passionately concerned, on the other hand, with comparing the COMPLEXITY of behavior."[7]

One of the essential elements of this *contagious complexity* was, of course, the notion of "retroaction." It is easier to grasp the convergence occurring between the behaviorist method and the assumed energetic aspect of the concept of data processing, if we remember the relative definition of speed: *"Speed is not a phenomenon, it is the relationship between phenomena."* When we bring both definitions together, we can see that they are identical and that if there is no "reality" outside the relationships between phenomena, then *the reality of information is entirely contained in the speed of its dissemination.* And so INFORMATION (matter's third dimension) is only ever *"the designation of the state a phenomenon assumes at a given moment."*[8] In other words, its "relief"—whence the current use after this of the terms "high definition" and "high resolution" in relation to sound and image.

CYBERSPACE, or, more exactly, "cybernetic space-time," will emerge from the observation, popular with the press, that information is of value only if it is delivered fast; better still, that *speed is information itself!*

There is one final point to note here: it was between the research centers at Bletchley Park in Great Britain and Los Alamos in the United States that the destiny, not to mention behavior, of our fin de siècle would be played out. The simultaneous inventions of *the bomb* and *the computer* would in fact perfectly illustrate the marriage of inconvenience between energy and information. The "microchip revolution" today extends the damage done by the disastrous fallout of the "macroenergetic revolution," so that we are entitled to ask ourselves, after the end of the cold war and the decline of *nuclear* dissuasion, what will be the future damage caused by the onset of the *computerized* dissuasion of perceptible reality, which is more and more closely tied to a veritable "industrialization of simulation"?

"When science has learned to recognize the value of what it initially rejected as subjective, this will gradually be reintroduced—though incorporated as a specific case in the relationships and objects that define the world as science sees it. *The world will then close in on itself,* and, except for whatever in us thinks and does science, the impartial observer that lives inside us, *we will have become a part or a moment in the Great Object."*[9]

The concept of the world as a GREAT OBJECT, denounced by Merleau-Ponty in 1959 as an optical illusion of perceptual faith, introduces us to the reality of the end of the millenium.

In Merleau-Ponty's phenomenology of perception, we find the idea Husserl shared that space is limited to the world of sensory experience and that beyond this there is no space worthy of the name, only the excess of a "time depth": universal time, which has nothing in common with the void of so-called cosmic space. But today, with INFORMATION as the last dimension of space-time-matter, it is very tempting for infonauts to identify this spaceless time depth *with information that is no longer restricted but has become generalized.* In other words, with an INFORMA-TION-WORLD in which physics and computer science would be completely indistinguishable.

The pollution of the far reaches of the life-size geophysical world through implementation of the absolute speed of information-carrying waves, has now capped off the pollution of natural substances—the air, water, flora, and fauna. We will soon see the *data pollution* of our world proper and, finally, of the astrophysical universe itself. The expansion phenomenon that big bang supporters are keen on will extinguish itself suddenly before the "evidence" *of the generalized principle of information expansion!*[10]

Once this happens, disinformation will no longer be concerned solely with dressing up the facts. It will also latch on to the reality principle to try to subtly introduce a new type of universe: *a virtual universe,* the ultimate form of an undermining of reality of cosmic proportions in which Newton's universal attraction will be replaced once and for all by the cybernetic domination of thought. *"That is how the Great Universe will one day use itself up,"* Girardi once lamented. . . .

How can we fail to notice that the imminent reign of computer-generated virtuality was made possible, indeed necessary, by the long-awaited advent of globalization? If the world is closing in on itself and becoming *a finite world,* according to Merleau-Ponty, the necessity of overtaking it becomes patently obvious. Where the *far* horizon of our planet's antipodes has finally become an *apparent,* or more precisely, "trans-apparent" horizon, through the special effects of audiovisual techniques, the urgent necessity of another limit, a new frontier, suddenly makes itself felt—one that would no longer be geographic but infographic; the *mental image* of far distances hidden by the curve of the globe yielding to the *instrumental imagery* of a computer that can generate a virtual otherworld, thanks to the computing speed of its integrated circuits.

Scott Fisher claims apropos, *"As the processing power and graphic frame rate on microcomputers quickly increase, portable, personal virtual-environment systems will also become available.* The possibilities of virtual realities, it appears, are as limitless as the possibilities of reality. *They can provide a human interface that disappears—a doorway to other worlds."* [11]

Once more a certain observation regarding the change in the speed of history comes into its own: long-term, short-term, *real-term.*

Fernand Braudel was right when he spoke of the energetic dimension of history, of time's speeding up. . . . If the tale of historical chronicles is effectively *written information,* it is also energy and mass—that of the living species.

The three states of matter are thus at work in our memories, and we will not be able to understand what has been happening for some years now unless we can see the connection between the two states of historical time: the "energetic" and the "informational." As time changes, it is speed that changes gear and history that changes camp, finally attaining *a speed limit that cannot be exceeded.*

The classic object of this twentieth century, now drawing to a close, is thus not, as ecologists have feared, the nuclear power station, but the particle accelerator. History is not just the geopolitics of peoples that have succeeded each other over the ages. It is also the implementation of the energy available in each particular period—formerly metabolic, then mechanical, relative speed, and absolute speed today with the boom in electromagnetic systems.

After the recent breaking of the sound and heat barriers, our era is the first to reach its cosmological speed limit with the breaking of the *light barrier*. With the corollary discoveries of the acceleration of historical time and the expansion of cosmic space, we are thus at last discovering their common limit. This has nothing to do with the specious arguments of Fukuyama and company, for it is not a matter of the end of history, but, more precisely, of history's upper speed limit, the *time barrier* merging with the light-speed barrier. As a Christian member of the resistance against totalitarianism once put it, "History is a dizzying kaleidoscope. The breathtakingly frantic pace at which events have been unfolding over the last quarter of a century favor the rise to power of forgetting."[12] Whence not only the infamous and sinister "revisionism" or negationism that seeks to invalidate events occurring from the Second World War on, but, more insidious still, the computerized undermining of reality that has today wound up in the defeat of the facts, since information now wins out over the reality of the event.

Having enabled history's TEMPO barrier to be attained, computing speed is now leading to the possible "industrialization" of forgetting and lack. Physicists claim that the speed of light, like universal gravity, is a *property of empty space*. If this is the case, then lack is at a premium and the indirect lighting of the light of speed will soon radically alter our understanding of time as well as of history. That disabused traveler Paul Morand once noted, "I miss the World; I feel homesick for each and every country." In the near future, if we are not careful, we will miss not only history and geography, we will also long to go back to space and times past.

"Soon knowing about space will be as useful as getting your driver's license," Wernher von Braun declared at the end of the 1960s, the decade that saw man land on the moon. There is no better comment, I think, on the cybernetic art that is now following in the wake of kinetic art in opening up processes said to be those of virtual reality.

To navigate space, CYBERSPACE, as one formerly steered a motor vehicle: this is indeed the great aesthetic mutation of INFORMATION technologies. To transfer to the immediate environment the control that until now was exercised over the "object," the engine of displacement—and this, thanks to acquiring a "fractal" dimension, not of space now, but of time, of *real time,* allowing an individual's proximity to be virtualized with the aid of a process that controls their movements: this is indeed the most astounding use of interactivity.

The recent innovation of the "computerized suit" that can generate a surrogate space around us, *a portable virtual environment,* points to future revelation of some "psychogeography" that will be based entirely on cybernetic energy, which will then supplement kinetic and potential energies.

Jaron Lanier, one of the promoters of this immaterial wardrobe reckons that, "When Virtual Reality becomes widely available around the turn of the century, it will not be seen as a medium used within physical reality, but rather as an additional reality. VR opens up a new continent of ideas and possibilities."[13]

Required to locate himself beyond screens that have vanished, in an artificial world peopled by imperative signals, the man of tomorrow will not for long be able to escape an environmental control that will dog his every step, much as a missile is pursued by enemy defense. . . .

Such an individual, *dispossessed of his shadow,* will not only no longer be at liberty to construct some kind of mental imagery, but the landscape too, the country of instrumental imagery that will wrap around him on all sides, will illustrate Artaud's suspicions about André Breton's movement: "*Surrealism was an elusive virtual hope and probably as much of a con as anything else,* but it drove you, in spite of everything, to try one last chance, to cling to whatever phantoms you could in case they managed, however slightly, to pull the wool over your eyes."[14]

Controlled to an unimaginable degree, the "new man-machine" has certainly materialized the cutting loose initiated by Futurism, Cubism or Surrealism. But now it is less a question of dissociating objective appearances from reality, from the artist's subjective interpretation, than of shattering *man's unity of perception* and of producing, this time AUTOMATICALLY, the persistence of a disturbance in self-perception that will have lasting effects on man's rapport with the real.

Campaigning for such a ghostly world, Eric Gullichsen and Randy Walser claim that "in CYBERSPACE, *there is no need to move about in a body like the one you possess in physical reality. You may feel more comfortable, at first, with a body like your 'own' but as you conduct more of your life and affairs in cyberspace your conditioned notion of a unique and immutable body will give way to a far more liberated notion of 'body' as something quite disposable and, generally, limiting.*"[15]

With that kind of talk we might well ask ourselves if we are not on the verge of seeing the process of "artificial" rather than "natural" selection of man's ocular imagery get under way: the image ERECTUS of (graphic) optics ceding to the image SAPIENS of (infographic) electro-optics. In other words, to the sudden superiority of the digital image over the image of the naked eye,[16] the search for high audiovisual resolution finally being explicable only in terms of *the endlessly repeated will to ultimately alter the rapport between the real and the virtual,* bringing us belated confirmation of Antonin Artaud's desperate observation about the immediate postwar period: "What defines the obscene life we are living is that all our perceptions, all our impressions have been distilled for us; we can now only live them one drop at a time, *breathing the air of the scenery from the top and to the side.*"[17]

Something is getting bigger, that's for sure, but it is not the frog in the fairy tale anymore—or the allegedly expanding sphere of a cosmos whose future now looks uncertain. *It is the eyeball that now englobes man's entire body.* Smashing the being's unity to smithereens, the fractional dimensions of cyberspace enable us to transfer the content of our sensations to an impalpable DOUBLE, suppressing, along with the old inside/outside dichotemy, the *hic* and *nunc* of immediate action.

This is where one of Karl Popper's most important ideas comes in, as developed in his study of causality and evolution, *A World of Propensities.* We should remember that Popper, too, has always enlisted in a cybernetic perspective. It was Popper, after all, who said, "We learn by trial and error, that is, *retroactively.*" In his latest essay, Popper presents "the propensity interpretation of probability" as a generalized dynamism: "The tendency of statistical averages to remain stable if the conditions remain stable is one of the most remarkable characteristics of our universe. It can be explained, I hold, only by the propensity theory; by the theory that there exist weighted possibilities that are *more than mere possibilities,* but tendencies or propensities to become real: tendencies or propensities to realize themselves that are inherent in all possibilities in varying degrees and which are something like forces that keep the statistics stable."[18]

According to this thesis, the statistical tendency becomes fact, becomes a FORCE, a force field, which we then have to reckon with. Popper goes on to say, "Propensities, it is assumed, are not mere possibilities but are physical realities. They are as real as forces, or fields of forces. And vice versa: forces are propensities. They are propensities for setting bodies in motion. Forces are propensities to accelerate, and fields of forces are propensities distributed over some region of space and perhaps changing continuously over this region (like distances from some given origin). *Fields of forces are fields of propensities; they are real, they exist.*"[19]

This is not too hard to follow. Popper's introduction of the concept of a "statistical propensity" amounts to a fresh generalization of the idea of "force" (or dynamism) lifted wholesale from the mathematical logic of 1940s research. By this very fact, the indeterminist approach introduces us to hypotheses about virtual reality. In the same work, published in 1990, Popper continues, "Propensities, like Newtonian attractive forces, are invisible, and, like them, they can act: they are *actual,* they are *real.* We therefore are compelled to attribute a kind of reality to mere possibilities, especially to weighted possibilities. . . . This view of propensities allows us to see in a new light the processes that constitute our world: the world process. The world is no longer a CAUSAL MACHINE—it can now be seen as a world of propensities, as an unfolding process of realizing possibilities and of unfolding possibilities."[20]

Such a vision is obviously related to the previously mentioned "expansion," but it is no longer a matter of the big bang. It is now a matter, rather, of the explosion of a kind of LOGIC BOMB that destroys the theoretical world of astrophysics by introducing the virus of a probabilist concept of reality not too removed from the perspective offered by the recent development of *general information theory.*[21]

With Karl Popper, the space of the possible increases. Propensities are properties of the global physical situation. Not only will the future be open, but the universe will be openly *unresolved.*

By way of conclusion, Popper further specifies, "In all these cases the propensity theory allows us to work with an *objective* theory of probability. Quite apart from the fact that we do not *know* the future, the future is *objectively not fixed.* The future is *open: objectively open.* Only the past is fixed; it has been actualized and so it has gone. The PRESENT can be described as the continuing process of the actualization of propensities."[22]

If we replace the *beau mot* "propensity" with the more mathematical *"statistical tendency,"* or even your simple "average," Karl Popper's famous open universe is already no more than the product of a hidden motor: *a logical inference motor,* a fresh *deus ex machina* analogous to the fifth-generation "expert systems" of computer science! Similarly, *present time* cannot correctly be described as the ACTUALIZATION CONTINUUM of History's weighted tendencies; it is the discrete advent of a *real time* that is itself nothing more than the outcome of a sort of general statistics of historical evolution, our *present reality* only ever being a reality effect, or, more precisely, a synthetic illusion!

"CYBERSPACE *is the result of a cooperative production of the microchip-based reality engine sitting on the floor of the laboratory and the neural reality engine riding in my cranium.*"[23] Thus defined, the living present philosophers cherish is hardly more than a LIVING CINEMA.

The horsepowered car was motorized with the aid of the synthetic energy of the combustion engine in the course of the transport revolution; the transmission revolution is now gearing up to *motorize the reality of space,* thanks to the digital imagery of the computer motor, perceptual faith letting itself be abused, it would seem, by the virtuality generator. Dynamized by the artifice of calculating speed, the *real-space perspective* of the painters of the Quattrocento then gives way to the *real-time perspective* of the computer cognoscenti of the Novocento, thereby illustrating surrealist writings of the 1930s: "One day science will kill travel by bringing the country we want to visit to us. It will be the country that visits us, the way a crowd visits some animal in a cage; then the country will leave again, miffed at having stirred itself for so little."[24]

From now on, the disabled person equipped with prostheses so he can control his environment without stirring has become the prototype of the able-bodied person *superequipped* with remote controls for all seasons; the latter will then try *to get the perspective of a* RETROACTIVE *environment to come to him,* the way you whistle to your dog. For this individual, the mobile advance of the human being will no longer consist of the immobile retreat of things before his very eyes. The reverse will happen: the mobile advance of things around him will consist of the immobile retreat of a subservient being, like a squirrel in its cage. . . .

Victim of the set, the CYBERNAUT has fallen prey to a synthetic illusion not so much visual as virtual, in which the visual thinking Rudolph Arnheim relished collapses before the misdemeanors of virtual thought, produced by an imagery entirely based on domination of the individual subjected to the mirages of *cybernetic ideography.* The new imperialism of instrumental thought suddenly unveils its PSYCHO-GEOGRAPHICAL IMPERIUM along with its "territory."

It is, moreover, revealing to observe the role played by NASA for more than ten years in the boom in virtual-reality technology. After numerous fiascos in the conquest of *real space,* the American space agency has ended up investing huge sums of money in research on instruments that may ensure its *conquest of virtual space's lack of expanse* in the near future.

On one hand, the construction of future orbital space stations already necessitated improvement in TELEROBOTIC technology; on the other, the very design of space probes meant new technologies of TELEPRESENCE had to be fine-tuned. NASA turned to the elders of the MIT team centered on Nicholas Negroponte in the early 1970s, particularly Scott Fisher, to produce the goods. But at the end of the day, the issue was primarily one of ensuring preparations for an identical exodus, *beyond Earth and Earth's concrete reality.* It was not enough for the audiovisual "unreality" created by the media just to do a cut-and-tuck job on our daily life. Infonauts had to prepare right now for abandonment of the material supports of immediate experience in order to exile us tomorrow in the immateriality of a new otherworld—*the goal being to colonize the void of a view-less horizon in the next century, by deporting whole popu-lations of consumers.*

Besides, collusion between the two absences of space involved in cybernetics and astrophysics was to be further accelerated by the role played by space probes in astronomers' imaginary. Skeptical about the usefulness of "manned missions" into sidereal space, cybernauts promptly backed the idea of sending "remote-control robots" as a more rational and economic approach.

Everyone agreed that TELEEXPLORATION would soon replace manned flights, and NASA even envisaged feeding its computers the flow of images the probes sent back to allow the experts to explore the galaxy *virtually.*

The Jet Propulsion Laboratory in Pasadena then stepped in with an experimental film entitled *Mars: The Movie.* Using data furnished by the Viking probes as a basis for an astronautical model of *virtual navigation,* Kevin Hussey's video anticipated exploration of the Red Planet, the film's avowed aim being to prod the heads of the American space program into firmly deciding to abandon the very idea of manned flight in favor of the less onerous practices of *virtual planetary exploration* of visual data sent back by the space probes.[25]

Thus, four centuries after the invention of Galileo's telescope, and thanks to the feats of teleastronautics, *the astronaut will travel in a room,* summoning to himself stars less subject to the effects of gravity than to the effects of the reality generator.

When cosmic imagery is completely digitalized in the next century by computer processors, cybernauts will be able *to travel in their armchairs* as simple televiewers, discovering a surrogate world that will have emerged from information energy. The big bang, a product of Edwin Hubble's calculations of the apparent speed of universal expansion, will suddenly yield its scientific primacy to the (transparent) speed of the infinite expansion of computer calculation! This explains the objective of the MARS-OBSERVER space probe, launched in autumn 1992. You will recall its mission was to thoroughly map the planet with a view to future colonization. But what is less clear is the nature of such colonization. Far from preparing a manned mission for some hypothetical landing of man on Mars, in the twenty-first century, the topographical survey of Mars's surface was intended *to make its virtual exploration immediately possible.* Whence the tremendous disappointment of the engineers glued to their control panels at the Jet Propulsion Laboratory's ground control center when the probe's signals suddenly went dead at the end of summer 1993.

By way of concluding this episode, a simple warning: if the electronic share-quoting system used by the New York Stock Exchange—their *trading program*—had to be applied to scientific disciplines in the future, "deregulation" would no longer only affect the financial products of the market economy. It would affect production of a new *metascientific* rationality also subject to the cybernetic law of retroaction. One might then expect the collapse, the *crash* of that instrumental reason Joseph Weizenbaum once denounced.[26]

One last remark: if rapid globalization of trade implies, as we have seen, the virtualization of diverse strategic, economic, and scientific representations, a formidable problem arises: that of the *precise physical location of the virtual object.*

With confusion setting in between the *real space* of action and the *virtual space* of retroaction, all *positioning* is, in fact, beginning to find itself in an impasse, causing a crisis in all position forecasting.

This "delocalization" also leads to uncertainty about the place of effective action, so that *pre-positioning* becomes impossible, which then undermines the whole principle of *forecasting.* When WHERE loses its priority to WHEN and HOW, a doubt remains—not about the effective plausibility of "virtual reality" so much as about the nature of its location and thereby about the very possibility of controlling the virtual environment.

Here is an anecdote that illustrates the *inventory* of a world that will from now on be lived in real time. A new type of watch has been on the market for a while now in the United States. The watch does not tell the *time;* it tells you *where* you are. Called the GPS—an abbreviation for *Global Positioning System*—this little everyday object probably constitutes the event of the decade as far as globalization of location goes.

Able to measure minute differences in the reception speed of signals emitted by two of the four satellites put up by the Americans, the GPS has now dethroned the SEXTANT by providing instant readings of the position of pilots or navigators using it, and it can do this with a precision on the order of approximately twenty-two yards—which will no doubt come down to less than twenty inches by the end of the century. So much for the capability of an object highly symbolic of the importance of positioning in the world, of cybernetic networks.

But what they usually fail to tell you in the publicity promoting the product—which has recently been acquired by most civil aviation companies and even quite a few national air forces—is that, in the case of a declaration of war against the United States, the Pentagon automatically reserves the right to tamper with what amounts to a "public service" by falsifying indications of proximity in order to guarantee the operational superiority of its armed forces!

NOTES

THE MEDIA COMPLEX

1. "Droit et journalisme: nature et limites de la liberté de la presse," an international conference organized by the University of Laval, Quebec, 25–26 October 1994. Note in particular the major contribution of Peter Desbarats.

2. Kafka reinvoked the apocalypse of the *Corpus Hermeticum* and the coming "monstrous marriage of souls and matter, those souls who no longer have eyes but only eye sockets with which they scrutinize, pry open and conquer; vision lost by the *indiscreet gaze.*"

3. Interview conducted by Philippe Gavi in *Le Nouvel Observateur,* 15 October 1992. On 30 November 1992, the French Senate decided to make nonobservance of right of reply in whatever medium an offense carrying a penalty.

4. Antoine Lefebure, *Havas: Les arcanes du pouvoir* (Paris: Grasset, 1992).

5. D. L. Cheney and R. M. Seyfarth, *Truth and Deception in Animal Communication in Cognitive Ethology* (Hillsdale, N.J.: Erlbaum, 1991).

6. W. K. Agee, P. H. Ault, and E. Emery, *Introduction to Mass Communications* (New York: Dodd, Mead).

7. Confronted by the threats of GATT, Jack Ralite launched a series of actions in 1993 against this seizure of power by the media, notably through the States General of Culture and the European Parliament.

8. Cheney and Seyfarth, *Truth and Deception.*

THE DATA COUP D'ETAT

1. Karl Kraus employs the term "kinedramatic" in *Nachts (By Night),* originally published by Herbst, 1918. See Karl Kraus, *Beim Wort Genommen* (Munich: Kösel Verlag, 1965), p. 340.

2. Many of the points discussed here are based on the following works: Charles Ledré, *Histoire de la presse* (Paris: Arthème Fayard, 1958); Jean Morienval, *Les Créateurs de la grande presse en France* (Paris: 1934); Eugène Hatin, *Histoire politique et littéraire de la presse en France* (Paris: 1859–61).

3. According to *The Iliad.*

THE SHRINKING EFFECT

1. "The Manifesto of Total Functionalism," from Adolf Loos's discourse, *Ornament and Crime,* delivered in Vienna in 1908.

2. Mallet du Pan, letter of 25 November 1799, concerning the mise en scène of the eighteenth Brumaire by Bonaparte and followers.

3. *Le Moniteur universel* (Paris: 1794–1795).

4. Refer to the "liberation" of the aerostat by Pilâtre de Rozier on November 21, 1783, as well as *Icaromenippe ou le voyage au-dessus des nuages.*

5. The validity of this chronology had already been questioned by seventeenth century pre-Adamite libertarians. See Franck Bourdier, "Adam ancêtre des juifs, non de l'humanité," in *Préhistoire de France* (Paris: Flammarion, 1967), on the speed of geological phenomena, pp. 77–78.

6. Pierre Assouline, *Albert Londres: Vie et mort d'un grand reporter* (Paris: Balland, 1989).

7. Dickens was a veritable *virtual novelist,* starting out as a *stenographer* (court and parliamentary) and going on to become editor-director of weekly periodicals such as *All the Year Round* (300,000 copies). He was nicknamed "the novelist of the road."

8. Unlike their Anglo-Saxon counterparts, eighteenth-century French men of letters were hostile to the press and showed profound contempt for newswriters. Even though he was a media celebrity after a fashion, Voltaire felt that *real intellectual debate ought to be conducted within a less ephemeral framework.* It was Emile de Girardin in the nineteenth century who managed to reconcile writers such as Chateaubriand, Planche, Constant, Hugo, Dumas, Sand, Maupassant, and Zola to the popular press. Later, in the 1920s, Gide, Simenon, Mac Orlan, and Dorgelès published exotic travel stories. In 1883, however, Hachette prohibited the sale of Maupassant's works at railway stations on the pretext that they *placed travelers in danger!*

9. Kraus, *"Nachts,"* in *Beim Wort Genommen* (Munich: Kösel Verlag, 1965). Originally published by Herbst in 1918.

10. The media's right to interfere is having trouble getting off the ground. "With unusual zeal for this kind of organisation, the International Communications Union (ICU) admitted a complaint by Belgrade at the end of April 1993 accusing Radio Brod of violating the Montegobe Convention—the 1982 agreement that aims at cracking down on pirate broadcasts." The *Right to Speak* was thus condemned to immediate silence at the risk of being stopped and inspected. This decision was finally deferred and the *radio boat against hate* is still broadcasting, but for how much longer?

A TERMINAL ART

1. Petrarch, *Mon secret* (Paris: Rivages, 1991).
2. "Exposure to Television as a Risk Factor for Violence," *American Journal of Epidemiology,* 129 (4), April 1989.
3. Paul Virilio, *The Vision Machine,* trans. Julie Rose (London: BFI/Indiana University Press, 1994).
4. David Fischer, *Le Magicien de la guerre* (Paris: Presses de la Cité, 1986).
5. Schopenhauer, "On the Suffering of the World" (chapter 7 of *Parerga und Paralipomena:* Grisebach).
6. We are still bearing out Plato's observation that every political regime engenders a new standard through filiation, democracy engendering the young tyrant who keeps to himself, on the watch far from the madding crowd and incapable of making friends. "When he was still democratically-minded and under the influence of the laws and his father, they [immoral attitudes] only appeared in his dreams; but under the tyranny of the master-passion, he becomes in reality what he was once only occasionally in his dreams, and there's nothing, no murder, no outrage, however terrible, from which he will shrink." Plato, *The Republic,* book 9, trans. H. D. P. Lee (London: Penguin, 1958), p. 348. [Translation modified.]

VICTIMS OF THE SET

1. René Gimpel, *Le Journal d'un Collectionneur* (Paris: Calmann-Levy, 1963).
2. Blaise Cendrars, *Hollywood: La Mecque du cinéma* (Paris: Grasset, 1936).
3. In the *Gorgias,* Socrates is shown dragging his bare feet around town, arriving late all the time and declared *atopos* by Callicles.
4. Seneca, *On the Brevity of Life,* trans. John Basore (London: William Heinemann, 1958). [Translation modified.]
5. Seneca, *On Moral Tranquillity,* trans. John Basore (London: William Heinemann, 1958). [Translation modified.]

FROM SUPERMAN TO HYPERACTIVE MAN

1. Nietzsche, *Ecce Homo,* in *Basic Writings of Nietzsche,* trans. Walter Kaufmann (New York: Random House, 1968), p. 693.

2. Honoré de Balzac, *Traité des excitants modernes* (Paris: Castor Astral, 1992).
3. *Art Press*, special edition, "New Technologies," 1991.
4. The first olfactory sensors have just been perfected.
5. Nietzsche, *Thus Spake Zarathustra*, in *Basic Writings*, p. 754. [Translation modified.]
6. Ibid.
7. Ibid.
8. Karl Popper, *A World of Propensities* (Bristol: Thoemmes, 1990).
9. *L'Autre Journal*, September 1992, pp. 24 and following.
10. *Art Press*, p. 29.
11. *Libération*, science supplement, 12 December 1990.
12. Barcelona twins, Marie and Theresa, had pacemakers implanted at birth in the autumn of 1992.
13. Nietzsche, *Ecce Homo*, p. 748.
14. Ibid., pp. 790–91. [Translation modified.]
15. Interview with Pierre-André Taguieff, *Le Nouvel Observateur*, 19 November 1992.
16. Interview with choreographer Merce Cunningham, *Libération*.
17. Jacques Jaffelin, *Pour une théorie de l'information générale* (Paris: ESF éditeur, 1993), p. 21.
18. *Bio-éthique, ville et citoyenneté*, ed. Cahiers du laboratoire de sociologie anthropologique de l'université de Caen, 1993.
19. Witness apropos the scandalous treatment of children in Latin America.
20. *Bio-éthique, ville et citoyenneté*, p. 12.
21. A French patent.

THE ART OF THE MOTOR

1. Theodor Roszak, *The Cult of Information* (New York: Pantheon, 1986).
2. In an interview published in the weekly news magazine *Die Woche*, Martin Bangemann, vice president of the European Community, claims that "all industrial jobs are threatened in the long run; there is no future in labor-intensive mass production in Germany."
3. Maurice Merleau-Ponty, *L'Oeil et l'esprit* (Paris: Gallimard, 1985), pp. 11–12.
4. From 1940, a team of British specialists thought to be able to break the code of the German ENIGMA machine gathered around Alan Turing at Bletchley

Park. The success of the operation, thanks to the COLOSSUS calculator, paved the way both for Allied victory and for the victory of the computer revolution.

5. John von Neumann, *The Computer and the Brain* (New Haven, London: Yale University Press, 1958).

6. Philippe Breton, *Histoire de l'informatique* (Paris: La Découverte, 1987), p. 118.

7. Ibid., pp. 129–30.

8. Jacques Arsac, *Les Machines à penser* (Paris: Le Seuil, 1987), p. 51.

9. Maurice Merleau-Ponty, *Le Visible et l'Invisible* (Paris: Gallimard, 1993), p. 31.

10. Jaffelin, *Pour une théorie*.

11. Scott Fisher, *Virtual Interface Environments* (1990), cited in Howard Rheingold, *Virtual Reality* (London: Mandarin, 1993), p. 131.

12. François Bedarida, *La Politique nazie d'extermination* (Paris: Albin Michel, 1989), p. 328.

13. Jaron Lanier, *Virtual Reality at Texpo '89* (1989), cited in Rheingold, p. 154.

14. Pierre Daix, *La Vie quotidienne des surréalistes* (Paris: Hachette, 1992).

15. Rheingold, *Virtual Reality*, p. 205.

16. Paul Virilio, *Attention les yeux* (Elster Verlag, 1992).

17. Antonin Artaud, *Lettre à Henri Parisot*, 1945.

18. Karl Popper, *A World of Propensities* (Bristol: Thoemmes, 1990), p. 12.

19. Ibid.

20. Ibid., p.18.

21. Jaffelin, *Pour une théorie*.

22. Popper, *A World of Propensities*, p. 18.

23. Rheingold, *Virtual Reality*, p. 132.

24. Saint-Pol Roux, *Vitesse* (Paris: Rougerie, 1973), p. 42.

25. A 1989 paper written by Erich Gullichsen and Randy Walser, cited in Rheingold, *Virtual Reality*, p. 191.

26. Joseph Weizenbaum, *Computer Power and Human Reason: From Judgment to Calculation* (W. H. Freeman, 1981).

INDEX

Compiled by Robin Jackson

PAUL VIRILIO is an urbanist, architect, writer, and professor of architecture at the Ecole Spéciale d'Architecture in Paris. He has published numerous books and essays. His works in English include *Pure War*, *Speed and Politics*, *Lost Dimension*, *The Aesthetics of Disappearance*, *War and Cinema*, and *The Vision Machine*.

JULIE ROSE is a writer and translator. She recently translated Paul Virilio's *The Vision Machine*.